Quick Guides for Early Years
Cognitive Development

Linda Pound

HODDER
EDUCATION
AN HACHETTE UK COMPANY

Photo credits:

Figures: 1.1 © INTERFOTO/Alamy; 2.1 © Mary Evans Picture Library/Alamy; 3.1 © Sam Falk/Science Photo Library; 3.2 © Silly rabbit/http://upload.wikimedia.org/wikipedia/commons/1/18/Skinner_teaching_machine_01.jpg/http://creativecommons.org/licenses/by/3.0/deed.en; 4.1 © Marmaduke St. John/Alamy; 4.2, 5.1 & 6.1 © Andrew Callaghan; 6.2 © Q-Images/Alamy; 8.1 © Jon Wilson/Science Photo Library; 8.2, 9.1 & 10.1 © Andrew Callaghan.

Orders: please contact Bookpoint Ltd, 130 Milton Park, Abingdon, Oxon OX14 4SB. Telephone: (44) 01235 827720. Fax: (44) 01235 400454. Lines are open from 9.00–5.00, Monday to Saturday, with a 24 hour message answering service. You can also order through our website www.hoddereducation.co.uk.

British Library Cataloguing in Publication Data

A catalogue record for this title is available from the British Library

ISBN: 9781444180572

First Published 2013

Impression number   10 9 8 7 6 5 4 3 2 1

Year   2016 2015 2014 2013

Hachette UK's policy is to use papers that are natural, renewable and recyclable products and made from wood grown in sustainable forests. The logging and manufacturing processes are expected to conform to the environmental regulations of the country of origin.

Cover photo © PhotoSG – Fotolia

Typeset by Datapage (India) Pvt. Ltd.

Printed in Spain for Hodder Education, an Hachette UK company, 338 Euston Road, London NW1 3BH

Contents

Series introduction

About the Quick Guides for Early Years series

This series of quick study guides is intended to support you in studying particular aspects of young children's development. While other books designed to support your study may focus on individual theories or theorists, this series aims to show how both theories and theorists come together in developing ideas and practices. While this process occurs in all fields of human endeavour, in no area is it more important that practitioners understand the relationship between theory and practice. We are working with young children – the future of society – and must therefore be prepared to reflect and adapt, while at the same time holding on to vital principles. We must, in short, come to understand why we believe and act in particular ways.

Each book in the series will include a focus on key debates within the area or aspect being considered. This will enable you to see the extent to which theory influences policy and practice. Sometimes there is a close match, but in other cases strong research evidence may be ignored or overlooked. Similarly it is hoped that the key debates will encourage you to think about the philosophy or theory that underpins day-to-day decisions about how young children should be cared for and educated.

In each chapter, key figures whose work is particularly relevant to the topic under discussion will be profiled. These profiles may include elements of the personal life of the theorist or thinker relevant to their work. They may refer to elements of their theory and may also identify other theorists by whom they were influenced or who they in their turn have influenced. Some of the figures, such as Piaget or Froebel, will be very familiar to students of early childhood care and education. Others, however, although less familiar may provide some valuable insights into the context within which more well-known theorists operate.

Throughout each book there will be reference to the research methods employed and to the practical applications of the theories and ideas under debate. A summary which might also serve as a guide or aide-memoire when undertaking assignments is also provided

No one book will provide all the ideas and information that you need, so there are a number of suggestions throughout of additional sources – books, journals and websites – that you can research to extend your knowledge further.

Introduction to Cognitive Development

Introduction

This chapter will clarify some of the terminology associated with cognitive development and cognition. There will be an overview of the way in which views of cognition have developed and an introduction to some key ideas that inform theories of learning and thinking, mind and brain. The chapter will also set out the structure of the book and an indication of the way in which chapters are organised.

In this introductory chapter, aspects of the work of the following key figures will be examined:
- Socrates
- Confucius
- Comenius.

Key debates will also be highlighted around:
- Holistic approaches to learning and cognition
- Cognitive style.

The development of thinking about cognition and learning

The term *cognition* is generally said to be concerned with higher level thinking and learning. It also involves activities such as attention, language, problem-solving, creativity, deduction and decision-making. The term is widely used to describe the mental processes by which knowledge is acquired through the use of reasoning, intuition, or perception. Views of what constitutes cognitive development continue to change (see for example Eysenck and Keane, 2010) but, within early childhood care and education, the terms cognition and cognitive development are generally concerned with the development of learning and understanding.

Metacognition or thinking about thinking is one of the factors that marks us out as human. Auden, the 20th-century American poet, attributed this to the development of philosophy in Ancient Greece. He argued (1977) that it is philosophy which has developed consciousness, which in turn has enabled us to become fully human. More recently (see for example Nisbett, 2003), however, there has been a shift in thinking – a recognition that while the Greek philosophy of Socrates, Aristotle and Plato may have shaped western views about cognition, views in the eastern world have probably been more influenced by Confucius' philosophy.

Profile

Socrates (469BC–399BC) and his followers

The date given for Socrates' birth is an estimate. He has been described as the father of philosophy (or the search for wisdom) and the most noble and wisest Athenian ever. Contemporary descriptions, however, are not always so kind – those writing at that time describe a bald and overweight man. After a period during which he fought in the Peloponnesian Wars, he dedicated himself to teaching young men – a service for which he did not charge and was therefore unable to provide adequately for his wife and three children. Socrates was elected to a political post but became unpopular through his questioning of contemporary values and customs. In 399BC he was found guilty of treason but rather than pay the fine imposed, or flee the country as friends suggested, he chose to die by taking hemlock.

His student Plato (427BC–347BC) suggested that it was curiosity, questioning and wanting to know what was seen as evil that ultimately led to Socrates' unpopularity. The approach adopted by Socrates to teaching through questioning is widely known as the Socratic method. It is this which Auden and others claim has shaped much of western thinking. Its oppositional stance, setting one argument against another, its reliance on questioning and logic remains the prime approach in our courts and our parliament. It was Plato who recorded Socrates' ideas – writing them down for posterity. In his turn Aristotle (384BC–322BC), Plato's student, developed and critically reflected on the ideas of Plato and Socrates. Socrates' questions were designed to elicit the truth since he held the view that knowledge is innate. Socrates and Plato believed that humans were born with knowledge while Aristotle argued that all knowledge comes from experience, especially from sensory experience. These two viewpoints are known respectively as *rationalism* and *empiricism*.

Confucius (Kong Qiu) (551BC–479BC)

The life of Confucius is difficult to separate from the myths that surround this still greatly revered figure in China. For example, it is widely claimed that Confucius died at the age of 72. Others dispute this, saying that the use of that particular number has a magical significance in Chinese culture and was therefore chosen to underline his legendary status.

Like Socrates, Confucius did not write down his own ideas – but these were recorded by his followers. He is believed to have written some songs but the tunes are not known. He too was involved in politics. He was exiled for a while but when he returned he set up a school. His approach, like Socrates, was based around questioning and on the power of example. They also shared a view of the importance of role models – it has been said of Socrates that he lived the life he preached; while Confucius proclaimed that greatness is dependent on leading an exemplary life.

Confucius' ideas have persisted. Tao Xingzhi (1891–1946), a neo-Confucian, was hailed in 1988 as a people's educator and a memorial hall was set up in Shanghai as testimony to his educational achievements. In relation to philosophy, Chinese thinking broadly relies not on argument but on consensus. Rather than challenging the views of others, the favoured approach seeks to come to an agreement based on the merging of different views. Nisbett (2003) suggests that this is reflected in eastern and western singing. In China, everyone sings the same tune, while the Greeks developed polyphony – singing a range of individual harmonies.

New ways of thinking

In the 17th century a figure emerged who was to have a major impact on the development of thinking about young children's thinking and learning. The life of Comenius interacts with other figures whose life and work were to impact on the development of thinking about thinking and learning – paving the way for the emergence of psychology:

- René Descartes (1596–1650), famous for the term "cogito ergo sum" (I think therefore I am), is known as the father of modern philosophy.
- Frances Bacon (1561–1626), an Englishman, was responsible for the development of the *scientific method*, which continues to influence research today.
- Jean-Jacques Rousseau (1712–1778) is said to have been influenced by Comenius and in his turn influenced the thinking of Pestalozzi. Rousseau was a highly influential writer and thinker but Pestalozzi, like Comenius, had a vision of education for all – rich and poor alike, working- and upper-class children brought together. Rousseau's ideas were more theoretical than practical.
- Robert Owen (1771–1858), who created among much else the first workplace nursery in Britain in 1816, sent some of his sons to one of Pestalozzi's schools. The ethos of

the school was to ensure that everyone could work with their hands and could learn academically – again echoing the views of Comenius. Friedrich Froebel (1782–1852) also worked with Pestalozzi and built on the work of Comenius.

Profile

Comenius (Jan Amos Komensky) (1592–1670)

Comenius was born in Moravia, now part of the Czech Republic. He, along with figures from many disciplines such as Rembrandt, Galileo and Milton, was one of the leading thinkers in what is known as the Age of Reason. Comenius was a bishop in the Moravian Church. His many international contacts meant that he was approached to take a lead in restructuring the Swedish education system. He was invited to serve on a similar committee in England but the Civil War prevented him from taking on that role. He is believed to have been approached to be the first president of Harvard University but was unable to do so because of unrest in his Church at the time.

Figure 1.1 Comenius

Comenius' approach to education must at that time have seemed revolutionary. He believed that education should be thought of as a lifelong process beginning in early childhood, and that women should have opportunities for education too. Schooling should be developed through play and through sensory experience. He introduced the notion of illustrated books for children and, in a book entitled *The Gate of Tongues Unlocked*, advocated teaching Latin through a child's home language. He held a holistic view of learning, believing that intellectual, spiritual and emotional aspects of learning were inseparable. He developed a philosophy, which he called *pansophism* (meaning that all knowledge should be available to everyone). It seems fitting in the light of these developments that Comenius has been called "the father of modern education".

Research Methods

Psychology arose from two major strands – philosophy and physiology. Philosophy, represented by writers such as William James (1842–1910), contributed the process of *introspection*. Consciousness was examined systematically through a trained process of self-observation. Mental life was thought of in terms of adaptation to the environment. The physiological strand contributed knowledge of the neurological system of animals and experiments with human senses, which also involved some introspective data. A key figure in this field was Wilhelm Wundt (1832–1920). In addition, a new science of statistics was developed by Francis Galton (1822–1911), Charles Darwin's cousin. This will be examined more fully in Chapter 2.

Continued ➤

Research Methods (cont.)

1874	Publication of *Principles of Physiological Psychology* in Germany by Wilhelm Wundt, known as the father of experimental psychology.
1876	Publication of *Mind*, the first academic psychology journal by Francis Galton in Britain.
1879	In Leipzig, Wundt establishes the first psychological research laboratory.
1881	Wundt publishes the first journal of psychological research.
1884	Galton establishes the Anthropometric Laboratory, where 9,300 people paid for the privilege of having their test results added to Galton's database of human characteristics.
1890	Publication of *Principles of Psychology* by William James in the United States of America.

Table 1.1 Key dates in the development of psychology as a field of study in its own right.

The development of theories

Ramachandran (2011) reminds us of the importance of metaphors in human cognition. As in every other aspect of life, the ideas or images we use to describe human intellect influences the way in which we think about it. Sternberg suggests that (1990: 5):

> by becoming more aware of the metaphors underlying ... theories and research ... (we) become more aware of both the range and boundaries of their theories with respect to the phenomenon they seek to investigate.

The mind has been described as a blank slate, an empty vessel, or a block of wax. These metaphors invite a very different response than when confronted with the mind depicted, for example, as a Froebelian unfolding of the blossoming flower. The "buzzing, booming confusion" described as the world of the new-born by 19th-century psychologist William James is a far cry from the social, curious, perceiving new-born described in the work of, for example, Colwyn Trevarthen, in the 21st century. The different images or models presented by theorists shape both their own views and ours – and in turn determine the research methods they choose. Similarly, Eccles and Appleton (2002: 320) describe theory as an "imagination machine", generating "questions and steer[ing] attention to the wide range of factors and phenomena" that should be considered. The thinking brought to the new science of psychology by different disciplines has inevitably shaped the variety of research methods adopted among psychologists since that time.

Holistic nature of learning

A term widely used in early education is holistic. Comenius and, in his turn, Froebel, regarded learning as holistic. Drawing on the philosophies of the ancient Greeks, Comenius emphasised the inextricable links between physical, emotional, social, spiritual, aesthetic and intellectual development.

1

Key Debates

Holistic education

Viewpoint: One extreme view in this debate is that schools are essentially places of instruction. Anything beyond the 3Rs (reading, writing and 'rithmetic) is not the business of the state but for community, home and family to take care of.

Sources: Encounter: Education for Meaning and Social Justice (journal – see: **www.great-ideas.org. enc.htm**)

www.infed.org/biblio/holisticeducation.htm

www.vernamontessorischool.org/images/Cosmic_Ed.pdf

Steiner, R. (1907) (1996) *The Education of the Child*. Hudson, NY: Anthroposophic Press.

Montessori, M. (1989) *Child, Society and the World*. CA: ABC-Clio.

Counter viewpoint: When compulsory schooling was introduced in Britain in 1870, the 3Rs were seen as being of vital importance – schooling was intended to create a workforce that could take urban jobs and pay taxes. There is, incidentally, a strong body of opinion that the 3Rs actually included wroughting (see for example: http://creative-blueprint.co.uk/thinkpieces/item/reading-wroughting-arithmetic) – evidence that the idea that education should go beyond basics has been around for some time.

During the 20th century many educators, building on the philosophies of Rousseau and Froebel, came to believe that educating the intellect alone was insufficient. Steiner's philosophy (known as *anthroposophy*) and Montessori's claims for cosmic education are among early examples of holistic education in practice (**www. montessori.org.uk/magazine-and-jobs/library_and_study_resources/teacher-training-study-resources/topics/cosmic_education**).

In 1979, an international conference resulted in the creation of the *Journal of Holistic Education*. The authors claimed that the 3Rs of education should be thought of as relationships; responsibility and reverence for all life. Throughout the 20th century, there has been a continuing tension between those who regard education as primarily intellectual and those who emphasise the transformative nature of learning and experience; and believe that there should be connections between all forms and areas of learning. They stress the importance of meaning and context in learning.

These ideals were never intended to be exclusive to early childhood education. Susan Isaacs and the McMillan sisters worked with older children but somehow the application of their theories became lodged with younger children. The ideals and aims of a more holistic approach to education can recently be seen to have made a limited reappearance in other phases of education. Their importance may be seen for example in the *Every Child Matters* agenda – although there are fears that this is itself being marginalised (see Barker, 2011).

Continued ➤

Paradoxically in a period when there is greater understanding of holistic education, there is also increasing pressure for the "schoolifcation" of young children's education and its "disembodiment" (Pound and Miller, 2011) – a return to basics.

Cognitive style or learning style

These terms are often used interchangeably but have rather different meanings. Learning style is likely to be the more familiar phrase, with visual, auditory or kinaesthetic (VAK) learning styles being those most commonly described. This view is often associated with Howard Gardner's multiple intelligence theory (MIT) (see Chapter 6). In fact, Gardner dissociates his work from theories of learning style.

Key Debates ?!

Learning styles and cognitive styles

Viewpoint: It is often assumed the identification of and labelling of children's learning styles can help practitioners to tailor their teaching to individuals, thus personalising learning and making it more effective. Various questionnaires have been developed to support this view (see websites listed below). The VARK website (www.vark-learn.com/english/page.asp?p=questionnaire), for example, suggests that "a learning style has 18+ dimensions (such as preferences for temperature, light, food intake, biorhythms, working with others, working alone)".

Sources: **www.bbc.co.uk/keyskills/extra**

http://brainboxx.co.uk/A2_LEARNSTYLES/pages/roughandready.htm

Greenfield, S. (2007) 'Style without substance', *Times Educational Supplement,* 27/7/07, page 25

Gardner, H. (1999) *Intelligence Reframed.* New York: Perseus Books.

Claxton, G. (2008) *What's the Point of School?* Oxford: Oneworld Publications.

Counter viewpoint: The notion of learning styles has popular appeal but too often there is confusion about what is actually meant. A number of very different ideas and theories exist:
- In the 1970s and 1980s, Kolb identified four learning styles (Kolb and Fry, 1975):
  - convergers, who tend to have narrow but focused interests. They tend to be good at identifying practical applications of their ideas.

Continued ➤

- divergers, who are imaginative and good at coming up with good ideas. They are interested in people and good at seeing things from a range of different perspectives.
- assimilators tend to be more concerned with abstract ideas than people but are good at creating theoretical models.
- accommodators are good at doing things and work intuitively. They are prepared to take risks and are good at thinking "on the hoof".

This work was criticised as being too broad and having little or no evidence of its effectiveness – perhaps because the way in which humans approach situations varies according to the context.

- Cognitive style, on the other hand, generally refers to a learner's habitual pattern of acquiring and processing new information, patterns of intellect and perception (Cole and Scribner, 1974) and is thought of as being influenced, at least in part, by culture. Criticisms of this work focused on the idea that some styles were less valuable than others. Lave (1988) demonstrated that most people use a range of styles. The focus of his research was on mathematics. When solving pencil and paper shopping tasks North American adults used field independent, or formal, strategies. When actually shopping, they used field dependent, or informal, strategies. Although the informal strategies used would have been described by earlier researchers as illogical, they were in fact exceptionally accurate. And this, despite the fact that they were often estimates rather than actual calculations. From these and other studies it seems likely that most members of all cultures can and do learn to use a range of cognitive styles involving both. Abstract and concrete thought are not exclusive.
- As a respected neuroscientist, Susan Greenfield (2007: 25) describes the labelling of children's learning styles as visual, auditory or kinaesthetic, as "nonsense", arguing that "it is when senses are activated together – the sound of a voice in synchronisation with the movement of a person's lips – that brain cells fire more strongly than when stimuli are received apart".

Nowhere is this more important than in the early years. If learning styles exist and if they are culturally moulded then early years educators have a responsibility to ensure that young children are learning to make use of all their sensory channels. Writing about the prevalence of dyspraxia, Addy (2004: 18) states that the early experiences of children with dyspraxia have often underplayed physical activity "in favour of visual and auditory feedback" – a further argument for doing all that can be done to use all available sensory channels. Greenfield (1997) also suggests that without movement organisms do not need brains. For young children physical action is the root of thinking and learning and, therefore, practitioners ought to be making sure that all children are kinaesthetic learners. But they also need to develop visual and auditory strategies.

- Howard Gardner (1999), whose work on multiple intelligences is often linked to learning styles, declares this connection to be a myth (see Chapter 6). He suggests that the term is used in a variety of ways and argues that learning styles, such as they are, vary with content. Guy Claxton (2008a: 48) makes a similar point:

Continued ➤

Many of the so-called "learning styles" are far less permanent, pervasive or clear-cut than they have been claimed to be. Unsurprisingly, people change the way they approach things depending on what it is they are learning... Also learning styles turn out to change and develop considerably over time. They are better thought of as temporary snap-shots of evolving habits and preferences than as life sentences.

- It could be argued that there is a possible use for exploring learning styles – to identify channels of learning that are not being made use of, and addressing gaps in young children's learning strategies. However, Claxton (2008a: 49) cites a study undertaken at the University of Newcastle, which states that:

Some of the best known and commercially most successful [learning styles tests] have such low reliability, poor validity, and negligible impact on pedagogy, that we recommend their use in practice should be discontinued.

In practice

The study of cognition has influenced and continues to influence practice. Swann (1985) argues that this application is not always well founded, describing the pitfalls of applying psychological research unquestioningly. In the chapters that follow, the applications of each approach will be examined in some detail. It will be well throughout this book to bear in mind Millar's words (1968: 18) that "theory does not have to be correct to be of use". In other words, not all of the theories explored in this book will have practical applications but they may still make a contribution to a developing understanding of cognition.

Structure of the book and chapters

Although the focus is on intellectual aspects of development, the interaction between cognitive development and physical, social and emotional development should not be overlooked. Equally the impact on cognition of the cultural context in which children are growing up; and their disposition or motivation to learn cannot be ignored. These are topics that will surface frequently throughout this book.

A word of warning about terminology! Cognitive development should not be confused with cognitive psychology or cognitive science – both of which are dominated by a view of human cognition that sees information-processing or computers as the most appropriate metaphor through which to understand human thinking and learning. On the other hand, the term cognitive developmental theory is most often associated with the work of Piaget. Keenan and Evans (2009) identify four approaches to cognitive developmental theories: that of Piaget; and of Vygotsky; information processing theory; and developmental neuroscience. While this book will endeavour to maintain consistency about the use of such terms, you will find that different authors and theorists use them in a variety of ways. Throughout the book an attempt will be made to clarify the meaning of these labels so that as you read other materials, the terms become more familiar and less daunting.

The next chapter will look at intelligence and its measurement (known as psychometrics). Chapter 3 will explore behaviourism, often known as Learning Theory. Constructivism and the work of Piaget will be the subject of Chapter 4. Chapter 5 will consider Vygotskian theory and socio-constructivism. Some consideration will also be given to other social theories. Howard Gardner's Multiple Intelligence Theory will be explored in Chapter 6. Chapter 7 and Chapter 8 look at cognitive psychology and neuroscientific approaches respectively. Although there is overlap, the two fields cover a large amount of current thinking about cognition. Chapter 9 looks at learning dispositions and the role of emotion in cognition. Higher order thinking including creative thinking, imagination, narrative and the place of music in cognition will be considered in Chapter 10.

Each chapter will include profile features of key figures as well as key debates that surround the theories under consideration. Additional sections will include discussion of aspects of research methods and relevant practical applications. Since this study guide is in no way intended to be exhaustive, additional suggestions for further reading will be included. A summary feature will examine key themes.

Next Steps

Pound, L. (2005) *How Children Learn*. London: Step Forward Publishing Ltd, pages 4–16.

Pound, L. (2008) *How Children Learn 2*. London: Practical Pre-School Books, pages 4–12.

Glossary

Anthroposophy: Steiner's spiritual science built on the relationship between natural sciences and one's inner world.

Cognition: the mental processes by which knowledge is acquired through the use of reasoning, intuition, or perception. Attention, language, problem-solving, creativity, deduction and decision-making are also elements of cognition.

Continued ➤

Glossary (cont.)

Disembodied education: a phrase coined by Tobin (2004) to describe the way in which young children are given less opportunity to move, to take risks and to engage with others physically, and how the brain is privileged over the body. Tobin and others (see for example Walsh, 2004) regard this as detrimental to the education of young children.

Empiricism: a theory of knowledge that believes that knowledge comes mainly from sensory experience.

Holistic education: an approach that claims that the 3Rs of education are relationships; responsibility and reverence for all life.

Introspection: self-examination of conscious thoughts and feelings. It may be contrasted with observation and was the starting point for psychology.

Metacognition: thinking about thinking.

Pansophism: a philosophy based on the view all knowledge should be available to everyone. It was developed by Comenius who believed that women should have an equal right to education.

Rationalism: "the philosophical view that regards reason as the chief source and test of knowledge. Holding that reality itself has an inherently logical structure, the rationalist asserts that a class of truths exists that the intellect can grasp directly" (www.britannica.com).

Schoolification: "an overemphasis on 'academic' provision for young children… It emphasizes the academic over the intellectual … demonstrating greater concern for the needs of the institution and society than for the development of the child" (Pound and Miller, 2011: 167).

Scientific method: term which refers to the approach to science proposed by Francis Bacon in the 17th century which continues to influence research methods today.

Symbolic behaviours: "a person's capacity to respond to or use a system of significant symbols" (Faules and Alexander, 1978: 5).

Summary

In undertaking an assignment on cognition you may like to consider making reference to some of the key issues explored in this chapter, including:
- the roots of thinking about thinking in ancient philosophies
- the development of psychology as a discipline in its own right and the role of statistics, physiology and philosophy
- the myths surrounding learning styles and cognitive styles.

Intelligence

Introduction

The term *intelligence* is firmly embedded in popular thinking. In many aspects of life the measurement of intelligence continues to play an important role in employment and schooling. In everyday conversation the concept of intelligence is littered with assumptions about what it is and what it means. In this chapter, the origins of thinking about intelligence will be explored, some definitions examined and some of the myths surrounding it examined. Psychometrics – the measurement of intelligence – will also be considered.

In this chapter, aspects of the work of the following key figures will be examined:
- Francis Galton
- Alfred Binet.

Key debates will also be highlighted around:
- Nature v nurture
- Intelligence – general or specific?

What do we mean by intelligence?

There are probably as many views of intelligence as there are theorists on the subject. Homer, writing around the sixth century BC seperated it from other qualities such as good looks, leadership or conversational abilities. But not all writers differentiate between intelligence and an "overall judgement of a person's quality or value" (Sternberg, 1990: 25). In the 16th century, the French philosopher Montaigne linked intelligence to curiosity, knowledge and truth – dismissing as unintelligent those who "by reverence and obedience simply believe" (Sternberg, 1990: 26, citing Montaigne). Huarte, a 16th-century doctor (cited by Calvin, 1997: 13) defined it as "the ability to learn, exercise judgement, and be imaginative". Hobbes, in the 17th century, linked intelligence to motivation, believing that there were few differences in intelligence at birth.

With the advent of intelligence tests, in the 20th century, arguments began to rage about exactly what was being tested. Boring famously pronounced in 1923 that "intelligence is what the tests test" (cited in Sternberg, 1990). This view had been borne out by the results of a symposium held in 1921 where many of the now famous contributors (who included influential theorists in the field such as Terman and Thorndike) refused or were unable to provide definitions of intelligence. Calvin (1997: 13) argues that many definitions of intelligence "sound like academics trying to define themselves", including as they do: "the capacity for thinking abstractly, for reasoning, and for organizing large quantities of information into meaningful systems". Put more simply, Piaget suggested that "intelligence is what you use when you don't know what to do" (Calvin, 1997: 13).

Changing views of intelligence

Psychologists' views of intelligence in 1986 were compared with those given at a symposium in 1921. The biggest change in thinking about intelligence was in the link between intelligence and culture. In 1921, no one identified culture as a factor in intelligence and its measurement but, by 1986, almost a third of the psychologists identified it as a component. This figure which would undoubtedly be much higher today following the work of Bruner, Rogoff and so on (see Chapter 5).

Today, intelligence testing remains a widely accepted part of educational psychology but there is a strong recognition of the role that learning dispositions, such as perseverance and motivation, play in intelligent behaviour. Howard Gardner's work (1983) on multiple intelligences was in its infancy 25 years ago but today is widely accepted (see Chapter 6.)

Implicit theories of intelligence

Both Sternberg (Sternberg et al., 1981; Sternberg, 1990) and Fry (1984) asked teachers for their theories about/views of intelligence. In broad terms, primary or elementary teachers emphasised social variables such as friendship and popularity, as did the children they taught. Secondary school teachers (and students) focused on verbal competence; while for college tutors the most important aspects of intelligence were higher-level skills such as reasoning and logic.

Carol Dweck (2000: 3) highlights implicit theories of intelligence held by learners and their impact on achievement. Learners who believe that intelligence is fixed (*entity theory*) tend to have "an over-concern with looking smart, a distaste for challenge, and a decreased ability to cope with setbacks". Those with an *incremental theory* of learning believe that through their own efforts they can improve their intellectual abilities.

2

Profile

Francis Galton (1822–1911)

Galton was a cousin of Charles Darwin and shared some of the same interests. He developed a vast range of research tools and concepts still used today. It was he who coined phrases such as *nature and nurture; regression to the mean; eugenics* and the *wisdom of the crowd*. He invented fingerprinting and questionnaires – as well as weather maps. In short, he was an extraordinary man, possessing, one must suppose, exceptional energy.

By a variety of means, he collected information about people's height and weight and developed the theory of natural distribution, sometimes known as the *bell curve*. This gave rise to phrases in common use, in relation to intelligence, height and weight today – such as percentiles and standard deviations. His interest in intelligence led him to develop tests of reaction time and sensory discrimination – which he believed in these early days of measuring intelligence would lead to greater understanding of its nature. However, Galton's application of mathematics to his scientific study of intelligence was "revolutionary" (Gardner et al., 1996) and contributed to the development of statistics and statistical analysis.

Figure 2.1 Galton

He collected data from 93,000 visitors to the Science Museum in London. The people involved were charged three or four pence each to have their "height, weight, hand strength, breathing power, head size and various psychophysical characteristic" measured (Gardner et al., 1996: 46). From the data that he carefully collected and recorded, Galton came to believe that children of, for example, exceptionally tall or exceptionally short people, would be closer to the average than their parents. He termed this *regression to the mean* and applied the same thinking to intelligence. Galton is often criticised for his interest in eugenics. It is suggested that this was less social engineering – rather an attempt to ensure that everyone had the best possible gene stock (**www.galton.org**).

Spearman, a later theorist, greatly admired Galton's work and like him believed that there was a positive correlation between intelligence and other personal measures such as height and weight.

Key Debates

Nature vs nurture

Viewpoint: Widespread dissent about whether intelligence is inherited or acquired through nurture has existed for centuries. The nature side of the argument may be represented through three distinct areas of psychological enquiry:

Continued ➤

- Evolutionary psychologists (such as Steven Pinker) conclude that our genetic inheritance cannot be gainsaid. Humans are from this viewpoint slaves to our evolutionary past.
- Twin studies conducted by Cyril Burt (1883–1971) led to the view that nature had a much stronger influence in determining intelligence than nurture.
- Arnold Gesell (1880–1961) established norms of physical and mental development, which he believed could not be accelerated through training but occurred as a result of maturation. The norms he identified were known as the Gesell Development Quotient (DQ) and were for a time used to measure intelligence.

Sources: Cohen, D. (2002) *How the Child's Mind Develops.* London: Routledge (Chapter 8).

Keenan, T. and Evans, S. (2009) *An Introduction to Child Development.* London: Sage (pages 15–18).

Ridley, M. (2003) *Nature via Nurture: Genes, Experience and What Makes us Human.* London: HarperPerennials.

Rose, H. and Rose, S. (2001) *Alas Poor Darwin: Arguments Against Evolutionary Psychology.* London: Vintage.

Counter viewpoint: The most extreme counter viewpoint comes from the behaviourist John Watson (1878–1954) who suggested that nurture is everything – that children start out with similar levels of potential, which is simply shaped and moulded by their experiences. There are, however, grounds for rejecting the idea that nature is of greater importance than nurture in this debate.

Criticisms of evolutionary psychology

Rose and Rose (2001: 2) challenge the views of evolutionary psychologists:

> To evolutionary psychologists, everything from children's alleged dislike of spinach to our supposed universal preferences for scenery featuring grassland and water derives from this mythic human origin in the African savannah. And, of course, there are more serious claims, such as those legitimising men's "philandering" and women's "coyness", our capacity to detect cheaters, to favour our genetic kin, to be more aggressive. Evolutionary psychologists claim to have identified and explained all these as biological adaptations – that is, behaviours that have been selected during human evolution to assist in survival and hence the propagation of our ancestors' genes.

Penn (2005: 71) mirrors this criticism, claiming that "what in other circumstances might be regarded as the most outrageous sexism has found an academic respectability in evolutionary psychology". Other highly respected writers and theorists (see for example: Rose, 2001; Karmiloff-Smith, 2001; and Gould, 2007) argue that our brains and lives are far too complex to be the "servants of our genes" (Pound, 2009: 44). Biological determinism would not allow us the brain plasticity and capacity for adaptation around which our cultures have been built.

Continued ➤

Key Debates (cont.)

Challenging research findings

Burt's twin studies purported to show that identical twins raised in different environments by different families have remarkably similar levels of measured intelligence, indicating, he argued, that intelligence was inherited. Burt's results continued to be relied upon well into the 1960s, despite widespread questions about:

- the apparently impossibly large number of subjects used
- the untraceable co-authors cited in his research papers, and
- the improbably perfect correlation in the data obtained.

Cohen (2002) suggests that "a hereditarian conspiracy" is the cause of the failure of scientists to challenge Burt's transparently questionable data. Data obtained from twin studies in the 1990s indicates that heredity accounts for around just 30 per cent of measured intelligence. Criticisms of Gesell's work have focused on the process by which he arrived at norms – omitting, as he did, from his sample of children used, those considered unusually bright or dull, those raised in poverty and those who did not speak English at home (Thelen and Adolph, 1992).

The impact of nurture

A range of studies indicate that environmental factors affect IQ or intelligence as measured by intelligence tests. Longitudinal studies such as those undertaken as part of the HighScope research indicate changes in outcomes through changed environments (Schweinhart et al., 2005). In the study undertaken by Chris Athey (1990: 56), a range of standardised tests were used prior to and after a programme of enriching activities. Athey found an increase of 27 IQ points on a Stanford-Binet test in the experimental group – gains which she claims "were not 'washed out' during the first two years in the primary school".

Flynn (2009) argues that IQ gains which he has identified in the population as a whole are due to: better nutrition; more education; more liberal parenting and the spread of a scientific ethos which encourages children to think in increasingly disembedded ways. Cohen (2002) cites a number of studies, which explore the impact of environment on intelligence, raising the issue of diets and drugs, which have been identified as possible sources of improvements in IQ scores, but suggests that the results are not wholly conclusive, except in the case of the negative effects of pollution on intelligence.

The intricate dance of nature and nurture

Cohen (2002: 158) also highlights some studies involving parents and underlines the fact that parents have a role in both nature and nurture. He writes:

> *Do parents who read more to their children improve IQ by providing a better environment? Or do children whose genes make them brighter insist their parents read to them more?*

Continued ➤

Sternberg and Detterman (1986) have attempted to clarify the vast existing range of views by suggesting that intelligence is located both within:

a) the individual at a biological level; internally or metacognitively; and behaviourally (academic, social or practical levels)

b) the environment depending on the demands that a society or culture makes.

The process described by a number of writers as a dance between environment and genes is explored further by Ridley (2003: 280). He concludes that there are:

> *experiments that show genes to be the epitomes of sensitivity, the means by which creatures can be flexible, the very servants of experience. Nature versus nurture is dead. Long live nature via nurture.*

Intelligence testing

Attempts to measure intelligence developed in the early part of the 20th century. Binet, with his colleague Simon, developed tests that relied on norms of development. In gathering large quantities of data, Galton had established the idea of measurable norms. Thus, Binet hypothesised, comparing the actual performance of a six year old on a range of tests with norms for that age allowed you to arrive at an intelligent quotient, an IQ score.

Profile

Alfred Binet (1857–1911)

Although born in Nice, Binet lived and worked in Paris. Following the birth of his two daughters in 1885 and 1887, Binet carefully documented their development. Unlike Darwin, who had published observations of one of his sons, Binet included some simple experiments. His reflection on these observations led him to develop ideas about the nature of intelligence. These included work on the conservation of number – later picked up by Piaget, following his time working with Theodore Simon (1872–1961), with whom Binet had developed the Simon-Binet intelligence tests.

Binet is credited with having developed the first comprehensive intelligence tests. Galton thought of intelligence as a fixed entity largely dependent on heredity. However, central to the work of Binet and his colleague Simon was the notion that intelligence could be changed. They were working to devise a

Continued ➤

series of tests that would allow them to identify children who would need remedial education, outside of mainstream schooling. In their view, intelligence was not inherited (Gardner et al., 1996). The tests they devised focused on more complex aspects of intelligence than those that Galton had devised. These included tests of "comprehension, judgement, reasoning and invention" (Gardner et al., 1996: 47) as well as tests drawing on day-to-day practical tasks. Simon and Binet believed children should be given a range of tests since, they wrote, "we can determine the intellectual level of a child only by the sum of the tests" (Gardner et al., 1996: 49, citing Binet and Simon 1916).

In 1914, IQ testing, developed for work with children, was taken up by the American army for recruitment purposes. Binet's tests were modified and renamed Stanford Binet and other tests, such as the Wechsler test, were developed – versions of which are still used today. The Wechsler Intelligence Scale for Children (WISC), for example, was developed in the 1950s. It includes tests concerned with general knowledge; arithmetic; vocabulary; comprehension; picture completion and arrangement, identification of similarities; coding and block design.

Key Debates

Intelligence – general or specific?

Viewpoint: Charles Spearman (1863–1945) proposed the notion of a general intelligence (*g*), which he, and many others, regarded as an essential part of understanding the nature of intelligence. Basing his theory on tests carried out on 24 children from a village school and 33 children from a preparatory school, Spearman argued that it was *g* which provided the energy to undertake intellectual activity. However, he did also hypothesise the presence of a specific intelligence (*s*) – a series of unique factors unrelated to each other and specific to particular tasks. Spearman believed that his data showed a correlation, or positive relationship, between different areas of the curriculum.

Many present-day theorists argue that there is a correlation between the results of most kinds of IQ tests – arguing for some general component.

Sources: Gardner et al. (1996) *Intelligence: Multiple Perspectives.* Orlando, FA: Harcourt Brace and Company (Chapter 3).

Counter viewpoint: Spearman's theory had many critics. Some simply built on Spearman's work – suggesting not one but several general aspects of intelligence. Vernon (1905–1987) divided Spearman's *g* factor into two, one concerned with verbal aspects, the other with spatial and mechanical abilities. These two areas were also subdivided into additional minor factors. Thurstone (1897–1955) on the other hand, came up with seven primary mental abilities, namely verbal comprehension, word fluency, number facility, spatial visualization, associative memory, perceptual speed and reasoning.

Continued ➤

Gardner et al. (1996) suggest that the correlation between intelligence test scores and school-based tests of academic achievement; number of years spent at school; and employment categories and status argues for some generalised factors. They also suggest that twin studies support this viewpoint. However, it is far from clear what the nature of *g* might be. It could simply be a measure of other characteristics such as speed or efficiency. Some critics argue that *g* does not measure anything specific. Correlation, they suggested, may not indicate a link. The fact that, for example, sweets and cakes both went up in price does not indicate that one caused the other. In fact it is more likely that a hike in VAT or an increase in business tax or the price of sugar is the cause of both price rises.

Specific intelligences

Guilford (1897–1987) developed a structure of intellect model (SOI). Presented as a cube, this model argues for somewhere around 120 factors of intelligence (for a breakdown of what these were see **www.mhhe. com/cls/psy/ch08/guilford.mhtml**; and/or Gardner et al. 1996: 70–1). Estimates vary because not all factors were fully researched. In fact it has been suggested (Carroll, 1993: 60) that:

> Guilford's SOI model must, therefore, be marked down as a somewhat eccentric aberration in the history of intelligence models; that so much attention has been paid to it is disturbing, to the extent that textbooks and other treatments of it have given the impression that the model is valid and widely accepted, when clearly it is not.

Sternberg (1985) proposed what is known as a triarchic theory of intelligence – described by Ceci (1996) as highly influential among cognitive researchers, rooted as it is in an information-processing model of thinking and learning (see Chapter 7). Sternberg's theory takes account of the context in which the task is being done, and how familiar or novel it is. It identifies three types of giftedness, illustrated by three fictional students (Sternberg, 1997):

- A for "Alice", regarded as having analytical intelligence. She is likely to get high levels of attainment in school but may have trouble at higher levels of education in graduate school because she is insufficiently creative.
- B for "Barbara", identified as having synthetic giftedness. She probably didn't do as well as Alice in school, but her exceptional creative and intuitive skills meant that she was likely to be drawn into higher levels of study and research.
- C for "Celia" who is described as practically gifted and therefore likely to succeed anywhere. Sternberg (1997: 44) describes her as: highly successful in figuring out what she needed to do in order to succeed in an academic environment. She knew what kind of research was valued, how to get articles into journals, how to impress people at job interviews, and the like.

———————————————————————————————————— Continued ➤

Key Debates (cont.)

?!

The Flynn effect

Since the time when intelligence testing was introduced, test scores have been steadily rising. It is estimated that on average IQ has gained three points every ten years. These gains have not been across the board – indeed, measures of vocabulary, arithmetic and general information have changed little. This of course could be said to argue against *g* intelligence. Many theories have been put forward as to how or why this has occurred. Flynn (2009) highlights earlier intervention; greater familiarity with tests and test situations and a more complex environment may mean that the brain is becoming more flexible and adaptable. Flynn adds that "today's youth are much better at on-the-spot problem solving without a previously learned method" than were their parents. He argues that this may be because memory and the speed of information processing have increased, or it may be that ability to think in the abstract and to categorise have improved.

Research Methods

Research methods are dependent on the view taken of intelligence. If the theorist believes it to be about response speed then methods will focus on that, but if the key elements are thought to be vocabulary or spatial awareness research methods will look very different. Tests or experiments of a very different nature will need to be created.

Research into intelligence was from its beginning closely linked to the development of statistics. The staggering amounts of data which Galton collected led to the notion of a *bell curve* – a normal distribution of results through which standard deviations could be set. Since that time, analysis of data has become increasingly complex. Psychometrics required a great deal of analysis – to find out what expected norms might be; how these vary over time; whether there is correlation between different tests and measures and so on. Much of the argument about methods and findings in this field hinge on *factor analysis*. Much of the work of theorists such as Spearman and Guilford was based on a technique called factor analysis. Gardner et al. (1996: 67) describe it as follows:

> Factor analysis is complex mathematically ... builds on the idea of multiple correlations. These are correlations between a given variable and two or more others – for example, between an overall IQ score and a test involving verbal tasks as well as a test involving spatial tasks.

They go on to explain that the variables are linked together as dimensions or constructs and it is these that are known as factors.

Continued ►

Research Methods (cont.)

The very complexity of this and other forms of statistical analysis often make it difficult for lay people or those without knowledge of statistics to understand researchers' methods and conclusions.

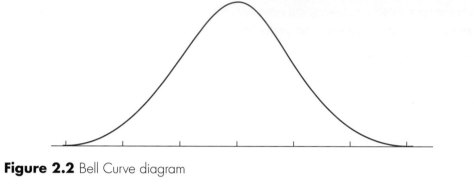

Figure 2.2 Bell Curve diagram

In Practice

Intelligence testing is used in almost every walk of life. Despite the many debates that surround the concept of intelligence and the efficacy of intelligence testing it continues to be considered of importance in many contexts. It is widely used in, for example, educational assessment and selection and for recruitment purposes. It is also used in many types of research as one means of selecting a sample of subjects. So universally accepted is the idea of intelligence and IQ that in writing about the impact of emotion on learning, Goleman (1996) developed the notion of EQ, an emotional intelligence quotient.

Next Steps

Flynn, J. (2009) *What is Intelligence?* Cambridge University Press e-book.

Pound, L. (2008) *How Children Learn Book 2.* London: Practical Pre-School Books, pages 23–31.

Glossary

Bell curve: normal distribution, e.g. with regard to height most people will be around the average with a few very short and a few very tall individuals.

Entity theory: held by students or learners who believe that intelligence is a fixed entity and that therefore effort is ineffective in improving achievement.

Eugenics: efforts to improve a species over generations, through encouraging reproduction of 'good' genes and preventing (or discouraging) breeding from genes considered undesirable.

Factor analysis: a technique used to find simple patterns and connections between multiple variables by conducting a series of experiments.

Incremental theory: held by students or learners who believe that through their own efforts they can improve their intellectual abilities.

Nature and nurture: popular phrase that describes the debate about whether intelligence is inherited or can be attributed to upbringing.

Psychometrics: the branch of psychology concerned with the development, administration and analysis of intelligence testing.

Regression to the mean: a common statistical phenomenon which hypothesises that the children of parents with extreme attributes, e.g. height or intelligence, will be closer to the average for that attribute than their parents.

Wisdom of the crowd: the view that groups of people come up with expert views. The concept was developed by Galton but is currently being debated in relation to politics, finance and so on (see for example Surowieck, 2004).

Summary

In undertaking an assignment on intelligence you may like to consider making reference to some of the key issues explored in this chapter, including:

- the wide variety of views of what intelligence actually is – a general competence or a range of specific competencies
- changing views of intelligence, including those held implicitly by individuals – professional and lay
- the measurement of intelligence and the paradox of increasing scores
- the link between inherited and environmental factors in intelligence.

Behaviourism

Introduction

Behaviourist theories of learning and cognition began with the ideas of Ivan Pavlov, and his theory of *classical conditioning*. The most well-known behaviourist, arguably among the best-known of all psychologists, Burrhus Skinner developed and applied the theory to education. Behaviourism is often referred to as Learning Theory, but should not be confused with all other learning theories. Behaviourism and Piagetian constructivism (see Chapter 4) co-existed in the second half of the 20th century. Gradually, behaviourism has come to be seen as too simplistic to describe the complexity of human behaviour and learning (Kohn, 1999; Claxton, 1985). Although still influential in education as a whole, the application of behaviourist theories lies largely in the field of special education.

In this chapter, aspects of the work of the following key figures will be examined:
● Ivan Pavlov
● Burrhus Skinner.

Key debates will also be highlighted around:
● Behaviourism and language learning
● Intrinsic motivation or extrinsic rewards.

The development of behaviourism

Behaviourism began with the work of Pavlov, experimenting with dogs. It continued in the United States of America. Edward Thorndike (1874–1949) is credited with developing the *law of effect* – the belief that behaviour leading to a positive outcome will be repeated. He also found in his experiments with animals that practice improved performance. John Watson (1878–1954) both preceded and influenced Skinner – who in the 1970s was described as the best-known American scientist of his time. It is Watson, a behaviourist through and through, who declared that he could train any child to become anything he chose – "regardless of his talents, penchants, tendencies, abilities, vocations, and race of his ancestors" (Keenan, 2002: 11, citing Watson). It was Watson who developed operant conditioning – by rewarding or reinforcing desired actions after they occurred – like promising pudding or sweets once the main course is eaten up.

Profile

Ivan Pavlov (1849–1936)

Pavlov, a Russian, was the son of a priest and he too studied theology. However, after reading Darwin's work he resolved to become a scientist. His main interests were physiological – in particular to do with gastric functions. Pavlov was a renowned scientist, revered not only in Russia but also in Britain and France. He became a Nobel Prize winner.

As he worked with dogs he discovered that if a bell was rung when it was time to feed the dogs, they began to salivate in anticipation of the food. In the 21st century it is difficult to imagine how important that finding appeared to Pavlov's contemporaries. Slater (2004: 11) writes:

> This [discovery] was as hot as the spliced atom or the singular position of the sun. Never, ever before in all of human history had people understood how *physiological* were our supposed mental associations. Never before had people understood the sheer malleability of the immutable animal form. Pavlov's dogs drooled and the world tipped over twice.

His finding was termed *classical conditioning*. An existing reflex, in this case salivating, was shaped so that it responded to a new stimulus – responding to the bell rather than the food.

Profile

Burrhus Skinner (1904–1990)

Skinner was born in Pennsylvania and took an interest in creative writing, poetry and the classics. It is said that Skinner read an article by H.G. Wells in which it was argued that the life of Pavlov, as a scientist, was of more value than that of George Bernard Shaw, representing the arts (Slater, 2004). Skinner then resolved to become a scientist. In 1928, Skinner entered Harvard to study physiology. He read Pavlov and Watson and, Slater tells us, began to build boxes, which would house the animals on which his experiments would be conducted. It has been suggested (Kohn, 1999; Slater, 2004) that

Continued ➤

Skinner's motivation in shaping of animal behaviour was control. While Pavlov had merely shown control of the dogs' salivary glands, Skinner is said to have sought control of whole living organisms.

Pavlov's research had focused on reflex action, namely salivating, whereas Skinner's interest was in shaping non-reflex, or operant behaviours. This became known as *operant* conditioning, or *instrumental* conditioning. Much of the criticism made of Skinner hinges on the fact that although his research methods involved animals, his writing focused on the application of his findings to humans. Skinner is most often associated with rats running mazes, but his experiments also involved training pigeons to play table tennis, a cat to play the piano and a pig to use a vacuum cleaner. In each of these cases it is not reflex actions that are being shaped, but random and in many cases entirely alien behaviours.

Slater (2004: 22–3) underlines the dual nature of the man:

> There is Skinner the ideologue, the ghoulish man who dreamt of establishing communities of people trained like pets, and then there is Skinner the scientist, who made discrete discoveries that have forever changed how we view behaviour. There is Skinner's data, irrefutable and brilliant, the power of intermittent reinforcement, the sheer range of behaviours that can be molded, enhanced, or extinguished, and then there is Skinner's philosophy, where, I imagine, he earned his dark reputation.

Key Debates

Language development

Viewpoint: Skinner argued, in line with behaviourist theory, that language, like all other learning, occurred through reward. In simple terms, children learn language because they are rewarded. Everyone is delighted when they begin to say "mama" or "dada" and thus behaviourists claim that children are rewarded and continue to utter those sounds.

Sources: Chomsky, N. (1959) Review of *Verbal Behavior* by B.F. Skinner, *Language,* 35 (1) 26–58. [This article together with Chomsky's additional comments can be found on **www.chomsky.info/articles/1967----.htm**].

Chomsky, N. (2006) *Language and Mind* (3rd ed.). Cambridge: Cambridge University Press.

Nicholls, J. and Wells, G. (1985) Editors' Introduction, in G. Wells and J. Nicholls (eds) *Language and Learning: An Interactional Perspective*. Lewes: Falmer Publishing.

Pinker, S. (1994) *The Language Instinct*. London: Penguin Books.

Skinner, B. (1991) [first published 1957] *Verbal Behaviour.* London: Copley Publishing Group.

———— Continued ➤

Key Debates (cont.)

Counter viewpoint: Noam Chomsky, also born in Pennsylvania, was opposed to Skinner's view that language, like all other learning, was learnt and shaped through punishment and reward. In a scathing review of Skinner's book *Verbal Behavior*, Chomsky (1959) made it clear that language could not be explained as the simple product of stimulus and reward. Children say and understand things that they have never heard before. They also, an issue central to Chomsky's argument, have an understanding of the rules of language at a very early stage – frequently overgeneralising rules – as when a young child may say "I wented...", "when I comed..." or "I seed two mices". Chomsky (1959) writes:

> Even a very young child who has not yet acquired a minimal repertoire from which to form new utterances may imitate a word quite well on an early try, with no attempt on the part of his parents to teach it to him. It is also perfectly obvious that, at a later stage, a child will be able to construct and understand utterances which are quite new, and are, at the same time, acceptable sentences in his language.

Chomsky went on to develop a theory of universal grammar, and to hypothesise that every child is born with a Language Acquisition Device (LAD). This view is strongly supported by Pinker (1994), an evolutionary psychologist with a strong belief in the impact of nature rather than nurture in shaping learning and behaviour. Pinker points out that Chomsky developed his hypothesis in an effort to counteract the behaviourist viewpoint, which ignores the significance of mind and brain.

Chomsky's challenge to behaviourist theories was further supported by the development of portable tape recorders (Nicholls and Wells, 1985). Brown and his colleagues were able to document the order in which grammatical structures were learned and to publish their findings in *A First Language* (Brown, 1973). These and similar studies showed some universal features of language development which point to some inherited features.

Research Methods

As indicated above, Skinner was influenced by contemporary behavioural theorists, Thorndike and Watson. Thorndike's discovery that any action with a positive consequence led to repetition (law of effect); and Watson's theory of reinforcement (that rewards following an action make it likely that the action will be repeated) both influenced Skinner's work. Whether teaching a rat to run a maze or a rabbit to pick up coins and post them in a money-box, his method remained the same. Actions towards the desired goal should be reinforced after the event so that they are repeated. By playing "with removing or altering the rate at which the intervals [between rewards] occurred, Skinner discovered replicable and universal laws of behaviour that still hold true today" (Slater, 2004: 12):

Continued ➤

Research Methods (cont.)

- *Positive reinforcement* describes the way in which pleasant consequences are used to reinforce behaviour.
- *Negative reinforcement* is the cessation of something unpleasant. If, for example, avoidance of electric shock is used as a reinforcer, the action that stops the electric current is a negative reinforcer. Kohn (1999: 52) adds that "contrary to common usage, it is ... closer to positive reinforcement (making a good thing happen) than it is to punishment".
- *Punishment*. Skinner did not use punishment – only withdrawal of positive reinforcers (Slater, 2004).
- *Intermittent reinforcement* is connected to *variable schedules of reinforcement* described below. Undesirable behaviour is less rapidly extinguished if reinforcement is intermittent rather than consistent.
- *Extinction*. In some experiments Skinner removed the reinforcer. Unsurprisingly, the learned behaviour (or conditioned response) ceased. Skinner experimented with and recorded how long it took to extinguish learned responses.
- *Variable schedules of reinforcement*. Slater (2004) suggests that this is perhaps Skinner's most significant discovery. He found that if animals were not always rewarded after completing the required task but only at irregular intervals the learned behaviour was even harder to extinguish. This finding is frequently cited as the reason why compulsive gambling for example is so hard to change. Winning provides intermittent reinforcement.

Source: Pound, 2011: 93

Skinner's approach to his experiments was controlled, creating controlled environments through the use of what have become legendary Skinner boxes. Although his experiments, almost exclusively, used animals, he also created a controlled environment for a baby – widely known as Skinner's crib. Skinner himself appears to have named it his *Heir Conditioner*. His daughter Deborah was put into this box for a few hours a day, which offered:

> a thermostatically controlled environment, [which] guaranteed against diaper rash and kept nasal passages clear. Because the temperature was so fine-tuned, there was no need for blankets, and so the danger of suffocation, every mother's nightmare, was eliminated. Skinner outfitted his baby box with padding made of special material that absorbed odors and wetness so a woman's washing time was reduced by half ... an environment with no punishing dangers (if the baby fell down, it wouldn't hurt because the corners were padded to eliminate hard knocks).

Source: Slater, 2004: 24–5

Continued ➤

Research Methods (cont.)

Figure 3.1 Skinner box

In Practice

It is easy to see the impact of classical conditioning in practice. You have only to watch a tiny baby anxious for food to see the impact that the sound of a spoon on a dish or being placed in a particular position – high chair or mother's arms – can have. Operant conditioning is used whenever we promise a sweet after a meal if everything else is eaten up. But it has been, and indeed continues, to be used in many situations.

The practical uses to which Skinner's work has been put include:
- training pigeons to act as missile guiders during the Second World War
- teaching machines
- star charts – in which desired behaviour is reinforced though rewards
- many approaches used in special education such as Portage, which breaks desired behaviours down into tiny achievable steps and rewards them as they are demonstrated.

Continued ➤

Some critics of behaviourism (see for example MacNaughton, 2003) identify ways in which educators use behaviourism to get children to conform. They question the morality of the way in which behaviourist practices enable teachers to "decide who we want the child to become or what we want the child to learn" and "construct an environment that directly and indirectly reinforces what we want the child to learn" (MacNaughton, 2003: 27).

Teaching machines

In 1953 Skinner had gone to an open mathematics session at one of his children's schools and noticed that the teacher was teaching children in a way (Husen, 2001: 59) "which, it seemed to him, refuted everything known about the learning process". Vargas (2005), Skinner's elder daughter, writes:

> In shaping, you adapt what you ask of an animal to the animal's current performance level. But in the math class, clearly some of the students had no idea of how to solve the problems, while others whipped through the exercise sheet, learning nothing new. In shaping, each best response is immediately reinforced. Skinner had researched delay of reinforcement and knew how it hampered performance. But in the math class, the children did not find out if one problem was correct before doing the next. They had to answer a whole page before getting any feedback, and then probably not until the next day. But how could one teacher with 20 or 30 children possibly shape mathematical behavior in each one? Clearly teachers needed help. That afternoon, Skinner constructed his first teaching machine.

Teaching machines proved very popular in schools for several years. The approach employed is still used in many simple computer programmes – count the number of objects shown on the screen correctly and receive a star or fanfare. As the key debate below indicates this may not work as well as Skinner believed it would.

Continued ➤

In Practice (cont.)

Figure 3.2 Teaching machine

Some of the practical uses of his theory to which Skinner aspired may sound more than a little alarming. They include his baby box (see Research Methods feature); and behavioural engineering (Slater, 2004: 15):

> wherein the power of positive reinforcement was used for the scientific control of humans. In Skinner's view this ideal community would be governed not by politicians, but by benevolent behaviourists, armed with candy canes and blue ribbons. He wrote a book called *Beyond Freedom and Dignity*, about which a reviewer wrote "It is about the taming of mankind through a system of dog obedience schools for all."

Key Debates

Implicit motivation and extrinsic rewards

Viewpoint: Behaviourist approaches, which reward certain behaviours, and by withholding rewards, extinguish others, are designed to support development and learning and to enable young children to conform to societal norms. These approaches work and are widely used in schools – in the form of gold stars, golden points and so on. They have been particularly emphasised in the education of children with special educational needs.

Continued ➤

Key Debates (cont.)

?!

Sources: Kohn, A. (1999) *Punished by Rewards*. New York: Houghton Mifflin Company.

MacNaughton, G. (2003) *Shaping Early Childhood*. Maidenhead: Open University Press.

Slater, L. (2004) *Opening Skinner's Box*. London: Bloomsbury Publishing Plc (see Chapter 1).

Counter viewpoint: Critics of behaviourist approaches claim that they ignore the complexity of human behaviour and learning. Alfie Kohn (1999) has been among the most vociferous of critics. In a book entitled *Punished by Rewards*, Kohn argues that praise is a weapon of autocratic control and that giving rewards, including non-specific praise, leads to less effective learning than no reward at all. His arguments are that:

- Rewards and punishments (which he believes have a similar effect) leave people feeling manipulated and resentful – which he suggests impede learning.
- "Rewards often reduce achievement" (Kohn, 1999: 59) because they reduce trust in relationships, a crucial element in learning. They may leave learners with the feeling that they are "being evaluated rather than supported" (Kohn, 1999: 59).
- Shaping behaviours through behaviourist techniques ignores the reasons for behaviour. It can ignore feelings, and emotions (Gardner, 1993). Slater describes her mixed emotions, following her successful efforts to get her baby to sleep through the night using behaviourist techniques (or 'Skinnerize' her as she describes it). Kohn suggests that the possibility offered by behaviourism to shape or modify behaviour in unethical ways should cause professionals to resist this approach.
- Risk-taking is an essential part of successful and creative learning (see for example Tovey, 2007). Kohn (1999) argues that the promise of rewards may make learners less ready to take risks. He gives the example of a scheme designed to encourage children to read more books. In practice, in order to get more rewards, they read shorter and less challenging books and with less attention.
- "What rewards do … is smother people's enthusiasm for activities they might otherwise enjoy" (Kohn, 1999: 74). Examples of children paid to do drawings or rewarded for drinking a particular milk product indicate that "extrinsic rewards reduce intrinsic motivation" (Kohn, 1999: 71). Additional evidence for this comes from a very different source. Claxton (1997) describes an experiment in which subjects were quite simply asked to choose a square from those in front of them, which matched a square that had been placed at some distance from them. When asked to pretend that they had placed a bet on getting the right answer, their performance declined. They were less likely to choose the correct square. Claxton's explanation is that they engaged in too much conscious thought, and felt pressured, when simply asked to pretend that money was involved.

Theories developing from behaviourism

Albert Bandura (1925–) has developed a theory known as social learning theory, which is based on behaviourism but which pays more attention to the social context and to motivations. In fact, so integrated with motivation is Bandura's work that he is sometimes referred to as the father of cognitivists (see Chapter 7). We might also think of Bandura as being to Skinner what Vygotsky is to Piaget! It should also be noted that, in 2002, Bandura was listed as the fourth most eminent psychologist – following Freud, Skinner and Piaget (Haggbloom, 2004). Like behaviourism, social learning theory recognises the role of reinforcement but identifies the fact that this is not always immediate and that the reward may not be apparent to others. Bandura claims that the reward that shapes or reinforces behaviour might be becoming more like others we admire.

Bandura's best-known work is known as the 'Bobo doll studies' but it is not without controversy. (If you are not familiar with these experiments see **www.youtube.com/watch?v=ICETgT_Xfzg**). Some criticise it on moral grounds, but others on methodological grounds arguing that hitting a doll does not necessarily indicate the same kind of aggression as hitting a person (see for example Holland, 2003). In addition, the role of imitation in learning is being seen as more complex than was hitherto thought (Rizzolatti et al., 2006) (See also Chapter 8).

More recently, Kahneman (2011) has drawn attention to the way in which context and intuitions, expectations and priming activities can shape our behaviour. He refers to a behavioural insight team (better known as the 'nudge unit') but his work is perhaps a far cry from the theories articulated by Skinner. He cites research that studies human behaviour in real-life situations. It is true that it takes more than simple rewards to shape human behaviour but he identifies particular strategies which change behaviour. Kahneman (2011) makes a number of suggestions about how governments can shape the population's behaviour by using particular typefaces or fonts in print; by presenting desired behaviours (such as healthy eating) visually and by framing the potential outcome of a particular behaviour as a loss rather than a gain. The jury is still out on this although Pinker is said to have described Kahneman as "the most important psychologist alive today" (Kahneman, 2011: front cover).

Next Steps

Gray, C. and MacBlain, S. (2012) *Learning Theories in Childhood.* London: Sage (see Chapter 3).

Pound, L. (2011) *Influencing Early Childhood Education.* Maidenhead: Open University Press (see Chapter 11).

Glossary

Classical conditioning: a conditioned reflex.

Language Acquisition Device (LAD): Chomsky's rationale for supporting his argument that a propensity to become a language user is innate rather than learnt behaviourally. The brain he claims carries genetic information in the LAD.

Law of effect: actions and outcomes are linked by rewards, given following the researcher's (or parent's) desired outcome.

Operant (or instrumental) conditioning: learning occurs when behaviour is rewarded or punished – though Skinner preferred not to use the latter.

Reinforcement: rewards that may be continuous; on a fixed ration; at a fixed interval or intermittently without a fixed pattern. Skinner argued that the latter was the most effective pattern of reinforcement.

Summary

In undertaking an assignment on behaviourism you may like to consider making reference to some of the key issues explored in this chapter, including:

- the value of research findings which were (a) based on animal experiments, and applied to human behaviour and (b) conducted in laboratory contexts, removed from real life
- the significant contribution made to understanding of language by the protracted exchange between Skinner and Chomsky. Their arguments triggered widespread debate and led to a great deal of research in this field (see for example Wells and Nicholls, 1985)
- continued research into the way in which human behaviour may be shaped – and some of the factors (including cognitive factors such as motivation and memory) which support or inhibit that process
- the ethics of both Skinner's and Bandura's work
- the many practical applications to which behaviourist theory is still put and the criticisms of those applications.

Constructivist Theories

Introduction

Although not the first to put forward constructivist theories (see Pound, 2011), Piaget has had an immense influence on subsequent thinking about learning and cognitive development. His theories have shaped our understanding of the ways in which humans construct knowledge. In his view, knowledge and experience are interpreted by the learner in the light of what he or she already knows, understands and has experienced. Constructivist theories within early education place considerable emphasis on children's experiences with play materials, the evidence of their senses and how they construct knowledge as they make sense of their world and experience.

This chapter covers aspects of the work of:
- Jean Piaget
- Chris Athey.

It also highlights key debates around:
- Stage theory, and
- Egocentrism.

The development of constructivist theories

Jean Piaget was without a doubt a giant on whose shoulders many other theorists have built, and continue to build. The fact that he has had many critics does not diminish the way in which he has shaped views of children and childhood.

Jean Piaget (1896–1980)

Jean Piaget was born in Neuchatel in Switzerland in August 1896. At the age of ten he had published his first scientific paper. He studied at the University of Neuchatel and completed his doctorate in 1918. Piaget became interested in psychology and went to Zurich to study under Carl Jung. He then went to the Sorbonne in Paris where he worked with Theodore Simon, developing intelligence tests for children. Simon and his team seemed only interested in correct answers, but Piaget noticed that the errors that children made at particular ages had a number of similarities. He then focused on the kinds of thinking which led to these apparently incorrect but pervasive answers. This insight was to lead to his stage theory of development (see Key Debates).

On his return to Switzerland, where he held a number of senior positions at the University of Geneva including Professor of Child Development, Piaget and his wife observed and recorded the development of all three of their children. This further shaped his understanding about the ways in which children construct knowledge.

Key elements of constructivist theory

Throughout his long life, Piaget wrote a great deal. His theories changed and developed over time and this sometimes makes it difficult to be clear about exactly what his views were. Key elements of his influential work include stage theory; schema and egocentrism – all of which are considered later in this chapter.

Through his detailed observations, Piaget identified several aspects of early development which convinced him of the qualitative shifts in children's thinking as they move from stage to stage. Issues which he considered to be limiting factors in their cognition include:

- *An absence of understanding of object permanence*: children under one year of age often fail to understand that objects that cannot be seen still exist – an understanding of object permanence does not yet exist. (For footage of babies who have not yet achieved a concept of object permanence, see **www.youtube.com/watch?v=NCdLNuP7OA8&feature=related**.) It should also be noted that although babies are born with an ability to track a moving object, experiments in which a toy passes behind a screen and emerges as a different object elicit no surprise in young babies. However, they are surprised if the object in question emerges from an unexpected place – apparently deviating from its assumed trajectory. Meltzoff (2004) urges caution in Piaget's interpretation (see also Chapter 8 for an alternative interpretation). He argues that since Piaget's time research techniques and insights have shown that babies' brains are much richer than Piaget assumed. Meltzoff (2004: 166) argues that:

> Human babies are special. What makes them so special is not that they are born so intelligent but that they are designed to change their minds when faced with the data.

Continued ➤

Profile (cont.)

It is this very mind-changing which Piaget alludes to in his theories of assimilation, accommodation and equilibration.

Figure 4.1 Piaget's conservation tasks

- *An inability to conserve materials*: Piaget's tests for the development of conservation went beyond that described above. He also presented children with liquids in two similar containers. One glass of liquid would then be poured into a tall thin container – at which children who had not yet learned to conserve would suggest that it contained more. Similarly flattening one of two identical balls of Plasticene would elicit the response that it was now bigger. In Piaget's terms the child relies more on appearance than on logical reasoning (Singer and Singer, 1990).
- *Failure of logic*: Piaget identified a number of aspects of young children's cognition which he believed were qualitatively different to those at a higher, more logical stage of cognitive development. These include:
  - Animism – children believe that things that move are alive. This may include the sun or a candle flickering.
  - Transduction – simultaneous events are believed to have a cause and effect link. The wind, for example, is commonly believed by young children to be caused by the trees waving.
  - Juxtaposition reasoning – asked to group similar objects, Piaget observed that children placed things together with no understanding of why they did so. More recent interest in narrative (see for example Haven, 2007) has shown that if asked, children will often explain their groupings in narrative terms. This may explain why children have difficulty in tidying up or sorting objects. Their reasons for putting things together differ from those of adults!

Continued ➤

- Artificialism – natural phenomena are believed to be caused by something akin to human intervention. A child is, for example, described as believing that God has three taps – one for rain, one for snow and one for hail (Singer and Singer, 1990).
- Realism or literalism – figures of speech such as "he kicked the bucket" are taken at a literal level. This is a feature of cognition among people with autistic spectrum disorder (see for example Mark Haddon's fictional account of how the world is perceived in literal ways by a person with autism).

Criticisms of Piagetian theory

Susan Isaacs, Piaget's contemporary, set up the Department of Child Development, now the London Institute of Education. She wrote widely for academic and professional audiences as well as for parents. Although she and Piaget respected each other, their views differed widely on many aspects of cognitive development. Isaacs disagreed with stage theory – believing that adult and child cognition differ only in relation to the different amounts of experience they have to draw on. She, as a trained psychoanalytic practitioner, also believed that Piaget placed insufficient emphasis on the social interactions and emotions that surround learning. His theoretical position was that play and imagination were something that children grew out of as they moved through the four stages towards abstract thought. This deficit view was at odds with Isaacs' view of play and is out of step with current thinking about the role of narrative, play and imagination in cognition (see Chapter 10).

Margaret Donaldson studied with Piaget and has done much to clarify his theories. As a post-Piagetian theorist, she has considered both the strengths and limitations of his theories. In the preface to *Children's Minds* she points out her indebtedness to him. Her criticisms of his work, she writes, imply that "no lessening of respect for the man or for his vast contribution to knowledge... No theory in science is final; and no one is more fully aware of this than Piaget himself" (Donaldson, 1978: 9).

Key Debates

Stage theory

Viewpoint: This theory is fundamental to Piaget's thinking about young children's cognition. He suggests that children are not just small grown-ups, but that they learn in a qualitatively different way from adults. Their drive to make sense of their world makes children active participants in their own learning, constructing their own understanding and furthering their own knowledge. Piaget developed his theory of developmental stages from observing that children of an equivalent age made similar mistakes and appeared to develop very similar ideas to explain their thinking. Piaget argued that, once young children's thinking had been provoked by new insights to move to a qualitatively different stage, there could be no return. The stages he proposed are shown in Table 4.1.

Continued ➤

Key Debates (cont.)

Sources: Donaldson, M. (1978) *Children's Minds*. London: Fontana.

Isaacs, S. (1999) [first published 1930] *Intellectual Growth in Young Children*. London: Routledge and Kegan Paul.

Piaget, J. (2002) [first published 1926] *The Language and Thought of the Child*. London: Routledge Classics.

Counter viewpoint: Freud developed a stage theory of psychosexual development and Erikson a lifelong theory of psychosocial development. Critics claim that stage theory defines children by what they cannot do. It is often referred to as a deficit or incompetence model of cognitive development. It does not take into account social and cultural contexts, nor the way in which development can be accelerated through experience. In different terms and at different times, both Susan Isaacs and Margaret Donaldson rejected Piaget's theory.

Isaacs believed that children were capable of logical thought at a much younger age than Piaget proposed and that the only difference between their thinking and that of older children and adults lay in terms of their range of experience. She offered positive descriptions of cognitive competence in young children: what they could do and how, rather than what they could not yet do.

Donaldson, writing much later in the 20th century, suggested that it was wrong to believe that the intricacies of human development could be explained by one age-based model. In her seminal book, *Children's Minds*, she outlines changes to Piaget's tests and tasks, which demonstrated that by enabling children to make 'human sense' of the situations, they were able to operate at a greater level of competence. For example, in conservation tests, a 'naughty teddy' pours the liquid or flattens the Plasticene ball – enabling children to correctly identify that there had been no change in the amount.

Bruner has proposed a theory of stage development (see Chapter 5) but rejects Piaget's idea that progress through the stages is one-way. For Bruner, we may move through the stages of cognition each time we meet a new or unfamiliar experience – moving from the physical (or enactive) through the iconic to the symbolic stage. He underlines the fact that we may also be at different stages in different areas of learning. Bruner also uses a German word *lebensnah* meaning 'near to life' to describe human cognition – a criticism of Piaget's tendency to over-emphasise the importance of logic over other kinds of thinking. This term also has echoes of Donaldson's suggestion that Piaget's tests did not always make 'human sense' to children.

Age	Piaget's developmental schema	Basis of knowledge and cognition	Description
0 to 18 months	sensori-motor	Actions and senses	At this stage the first use of symbols, including the beginnings of language begin to emerge.

Age	Piaget's developmental schema	Basis of knowledge and cognition	Description
18 months to 7 years	pre-operational	Use of symbols, abstract concepts, attempts at logic, egocentric understanding	The use of symbolism and pretend play enables children to explore a wide range of abstract concepts. Piaget described thinking at this stage as egocentric (see key debate).
7 to 11 years	concrete operational	Categorisation, basic logic	This stage represents a major shift in thinking. Mental operations such as categorising, use of number and early scientific concepts such as conservation emerge.
11 years to adulthood	formal operations	Master logical thought, manipulate abstract ideas, make and test hypotheses	At this stage children are regarded as able to deal with increasingly complex and abstract ideas.

Table 4.1 Stages of development proposed by Piaget

Profile

Chris Athey (1924–2011)

Chris Athey was a principal lecturer at what was then known as Froebel Institute (now part of Roehampton University). During her time there she set up a research project, which aimed to examine the development of thought in young children. Her research assistant on the project was Tina Bruce who has subsequently made Chris Athey's findings highly accessible and more widely understood among early childhood professionals. Athey offered an experimental group of children enriching experiences and documented the ways in which they represented their experiences. She analysed the observations of play, the drawing and models, and the talk that emerged from the enriching experiences, which included things like visits to the seaside or to a circus.

Schema

The most influential aspect of Athey's work is around schema. Piaget proposed that young children construct their understanding of the world through their use of schemas (sometimes known as schemes or schemata). Schemas are the building blocks of concepts. We continue to develop concepts throughout

Continued ➤

Profile (cont.)

our lives since our ideas and understandings are constantly modified by our experiences. In young children these changes are very marked because their experience is by definition limited.

During the first two years of life, which Piaget called the sensori-motor stage, the prevailing schemas are physical. Babies and toddlers use their physical skills to explore and all their senses provide vital channels of information. Piaget proposed that, from about 18–24 months of age, toddlers develop schemas that go beyond physical sensation and are linked to actions.

Learning, he suggested, occurs through three processes of adaptation – *assimilation, accommodation* and *equilibration*. At any age or stage, when we experience something new, we *assimilate* the new idea or action into our existing schema. The new idea stands alongside existing ideas.

For an example of this consider Piaget's conservation of quantity test. Two lines of an equal number of coins or sweets are shown to a child. The child is asked which line has more and has no difficulty in saying that they are the same. The researcher spreads out one of the lines and then asks again which line has more. Children at a pre-operational stage will say that the longer line has more. (There is a video which shows a child doing this – she actually counts the number in each line but still says the longer one has more. See **www.youtube.com/watch?v=whT6w2jrWbA**.) The explanation offered in Piagetian terms is that the child has a schema related to number and a schema related to length. These two ideas are assimilated in parallel but have not been made to fit together, or *accommodated*. The visual (length of the rows) takes precedence over the abstract (number of counters). Once the child has accommodated these two schema or building blocks he or she will have no difficulty in saying that the two lines have the same number. This happens as the child experiences some discomfort (or *disequilibration*). *Accommodation* occurs as a result of the mind's desire for *equilibration*. The discomfort often arises as a child (or indeed an adult) tries things out or thinks out loud. Think about young children building a bridge with blocks – early efforts do not include any means for getting on to the bridge but gradually thinking shifts and new ideas are accommodated. Piaget proposed that children's desire to make sense of their world means that once the inconsistency is identified, children, in an effort to achieve equilibration, abandon schema that in the light of new information no longer make sense.

In the 1970s and 1980s Athey used Piaget's term *schema* to describe the repeated actions of young children. Since that time her work has had a wide influence on practice in early years settings throughout Britain and beyond. Athey and her team identified a number of common features or what she termed schema – drawing on Piagetian theory – or repeated actions. These have become highly familiar to many early years practitioners and included things like vertical and rotational schema as well as enclosure and transporting. In analysing the representations, Athey identified four stages of thinking, which emerge as children explore schema.

———————————————————————————————— Continued ➤

Stage of thinking	Description
A period of physical action, where no clear meaning is attached	The child demonstrates an interest in twirling around, or running around circular objects
Schema is used to symbolise something	The child may play at being a horse on a roundabout he or she went on at the seaside
Exploration of the relationship between two schema or ideas	At the seaside, the child noticed someone fishing and is interested in the way in which the rotation of the reel made the fishing line longer or shorter
Schema supports thinking	The child becomes able to express these ideas in words and to reason or engage in sustained conversation about them.

Table 4.2 Athey's four stages of thinking

Key Debates

Egocentrism

Viewpoint: Piaget described children in the pre-operational stage of development as egocentric. He proposed that very young children were egocentric and therefore unable to decentre – or see things from alternative perspectives. It is generally agreed that he did not intend to use the term in the way in which it is popularly used today – implying selfishness. Today it is generally believed that Piaget was suggesting that young children were only able to make sense of the world from their own perspective.

Sources: Donaldson, M. (1978) *Children's Minds*. London: Fontana.

Flavell, J., Green, F. and Flavell, E. (1990) 'Developmental Changes in Young Children's Knowledge about the Mind', *Cognitive Development*, 5 (1): 1–27 January.

Piaget, J. and Inhelder, B. (2007) [first published 1957] *The Child's Conception of Space*. London: WW Norton and Co.

Counter viewpoint: Piaget's interpretation of egocentrism is by no means accepted by all. Many critics are unhappy about the way in which this interpretation of his results conflates spatial perspectives with emotional ones. Many reject the idea that tasks related to spatial concepts have any bearing on whether children are able to take on the thoughts or feelings of others. The work of Flavell et al. (1990) suggests that in complex situations children are more likely to revert to using their own perspective – but that this is often true of adults as well.

Continued ➤

Key Debates (cont.)

Donaldson, working with Martin Hughes, devised tasks which demonstrated that where situations made "human sense" to children they were able to decentre. Hughes used toys representing a naughty boy hiding from a policeman and children considerably younger than seven years of age were able to identify places on a board of streets and houses where the policemen would be unable to see the boy.

More recent studies of babies also indicate that very young children are able to empathise with others. They may cry when another baby cries, offer a tissue to a crying or injured adult. Gopnik et al. (1999: 39) modify this view by relating it to theory of mind, suggesting that very young babies don't have a complete lack of egocentrism since "real empathy isn't just about knowing that other people feel the same way you do: it's about knowing that they don't feel the same way you do and caring anyway".

This point of view is linked to work relating to the development of 'theory of mind'. This theory is based on what are sometimes called false belief studies (Cohen, 2002). A typical example of these studies involves two dolls or puppets. One of the dolls places an object such as a piece of chocolate or a biscuit in a particular box or cupboard. The second doll or puppet, without the knowledge of the first puppet, replaces the object in a different place. The child is then asked where the first doll or puppet will look for the chocolate or biscuit. While three-year-olds believed that the first doll or puppet would look in the last hiding place — despite not knowing that it had been moved — four-year-olds had no difficulty in identifying the fact that the first doll or puppet would look in the original hiding place.

Bartsch and Wellman (1995) propose a different development of children's understanding of others' perspectives. They argue that by four years of age, children are able to take another's viewpoint in a way that neither Piaget nor Vygotsky would have considered possible (Cohen, 2002).

Research Methods

Piaget's research team at Geneva, from the late 1920s onwards, undertook a series of experimental studies designed to test Piaget's propositions about what children understood at different ages. The research methods developed have been both praised and criticised. They are regarded by some as representing a great achievement in our understanding of young children's thinking and development.

For others, including his contemporary Susan Isaacs, his methods, which involved a form of laboratory testing, could not hope to uncover children's true competences. This criticism also drives Margaret Donaldson's work. Although she admired much of what Piaget achieved she suggests that his questions often failed to make 'human sense' to children.

Continued ➤

Tasks

The task, for example, that he used to investigate and demonstrate that children held an egocentric point of view involved a model of three mountains – which might have made human sense to Swiss children. Children sitting on one side of a model were asked to choose from one of several pictures or views of the mountains the one which they believed would be that of a doll placed on the other side of the model. The model included a number of features such as a house, which could only be seen from a particular point. Despite such clues, up to the age of about seven children generally selected whichever view they themselves had of the mountains. (To see a version of this task go to **www.youtube.com/watch?v=P7w8YxDbdiA**. Piaget would have presented this differently than the presenter shown on the video, but the sequence does give some idea of what children were being asked to do.) This task is sometimes criticised as demanding understanding of many layers of symbolisation – model mountains and pictures of them.

Questions

Much has been written about Piaget's use of questions in his research. Martin Hughes and Robert Grieve devised some ingenious experiments (Hughes and Grieve, 1983), which demonstrated that very young children feel that if an adult asks a question there must be an answer. When asked, for example, if red is wider than yellow, they would give determined answers – trying in effect to make sense not only of the question but of the whole situation.

In Practice

Piaget's insistence that children constructed their own understanding and were active learners led him to emphasise that adults should create environments in which children could discover for themselves. This approach has sometimes been interpreted within early years practice that "learning through play" means a strictly non-interventionist role for adults and this has played a significant part in the development of pedagogy in the early years. Margaret Donaldson's repeated insistence on the respect that is due to children and their drive to make "human sense" has perhaps, paradoxically, raised awareness of the complexities of thought with which children deal. Piaget's experiments have made practitioners more aware of the importance of what children say and how they say it.

In building on Piaget's theories, Athey (1990) has highlighted enhanced understanding of the way in which physical action underpins thought and enhanced practitioners' awareness of the practical applications of schema theory. Identifying the implications for practice of children's repeated schematic

Continued ➤

In Practice (cont.)

behaviours such as rotational or enveloping schema has transformed practice in many early years settings, especially those working with the youngest children.

Figure 4.2 A child involved in schematic play

As a result of their reading of Piagetian theory, many teachers came to believe that "readiness" for learning was something that could not be hurried. There is a tension between this point of view and the alternative, which proposes an earlier and earlier start to formal teaching, what Katz (2011) refers to as "push-down" effect. In addition, practitioners should be aware of the view of social-constructivists, such as Rogoff (2003), that children become ready through experience. This is countered by the view of researchers and writers such as Palmer (2011) and Suggate (2011) that there is little point teaching early something like reading which can be learnt more easily and effectively at a later stage. As Katz (2011: 125) suggests "introduction to formal academic instruction too early, and too intensely, may result in children learning the academic details, but at the expense of the dispositions to use them".

Next Steps

Knowing the background to Piaget and constructivist theories you can extend your knowledge by reading contemporary theorists who have built on his ideas.

Athey, C. (1990) *Extending Thought in Young Children.* London: Paul Chapman.

Bruce, T. (2011) *Early Childhood Education* (4th ed.). London: Hodder.

Cohen, D. (2002) *How the Child's Mind Develops.* London: Routledge.

Nutbrown, C. (2011) *Threads of thinking* (4th ed.). London: Sage.

Glossary

Adaptation: Piaget's theory of how children's schemas change in response to experiences: through assimilation, accommodation and the drive for equilibration.

Deficit or incompetence model: an approach that focuses more on what children cannot yet do, rather than on their current level of competence.

Egocentrism: within Piaget's theory young children could only make sense of the world from their own perspective and were unable to take alternative perspectives into account.

Schemas: repeated patterns of behaviour that characterise how children explore and understand their world at a given time.

Stage theory: an explanatory approach that proposes there are distinct stages of development through which all children pass in the same sequence. Piaget termed this a "genetic epistemology": a timetable established by nature for the four stages of cognitive development.

Summary

In undertaking an assignment on constructivist theories you may like to consider making reference to some of the key issues explored in this chapter, including:

- the unique and highly significant contribution to our understanding of cognition of Piaget's theories
- the way in which concepts such as stage theory and egocentrism have led to new insights and are key elements in the development of new theories, including the development of social constructivism
- the widespread view that Piaget under-emphasised social and emotional aspects of cognition, while overestimating logical and mathematical thinking
- the implications of Athey's study of schema for practice in the early years
- the importance of Piaget's contribution to research methods. His use of detailed observation has contributed a great deal to research into cognition. Although his detailed research methods have been criticised, they promoted new ways of investigating children's understanding.

Socio-cultural Theories and Social Constructivism

Introduction

In this chapter the work of another famous constructivist, Lev Vygotsky, will be explored. His work differs from that of Piaget, in that he was a social constructivist, identifying the social motives of learners. Vygotsky is, of course, not the only theorist to take an interest in the social aspects of learning and cognition. Just as Bandura's social learning theory developed out of behaviourist theories, we might consider a link between social constructivism and the ecological systems theory of Urie Bronfenbrenner, which is also included in this chapter.

It should be noted, in passing, that social constructivism means something different from social constructionism – although you may well see both in the relevant literature. The latter refers to things that are made as a result of social cooperation whereas social constructivism refers to individuals constructing learning for themselves within a social context.

This chapter covers aspects of the work of:
- Urie Bronfenbrenner
- Lev Vygotsky
- Jerome Bruner.

It also highlights key debates around:
- Language and thought
- Effective schooling.

Lev Vygotsky (1896–1934)

Vygotsky was born in Belarus, in the same year as Piaget. Although Jewish, Vygotsky entered Moscow University, where just three per cent of places were available to Jews. There, from 1913–17, he initially studied medicine but after just one term switched to studying law. While studying in Moscow he undertook parallel courses at another university in history, literature and philosophy. He subsequently became a teacher – which he seems not to have enjoyed. However, he soon became a lecturer at a teachers' training college, lecturing in psychology and focusing on the education of children with physical disabilities. By the age of 28, Vygotsky had become a research fellow at the Moscow Institute of Psychology. Having suffered ill-health for many years, Vygotsky died in 1934. It has been suggested that his early death has given him an overly romantic image (Cohen, 2002; Burman, 1994).

Vygotsky's theory of social constructivism

Like Piaget, Vygotsky was a constructivist. Both believed that learning occurs through experience; that knowledge is constructed by the learner; and that the processes involved in learning are of greater importance than the product. In short, "they were more concerned with how a child arrived at their solution to a problem than the answer" (Gray and MacBlain, 2012: 87). Both regarded children as powerful participants in the learning process. Gray and MacBlain (2012) also highlight the importance in both sets of theories of cognitive conflict to learning. What Piaget termed "disequilibriation" spurs the child on to reduce the uneasiness, which occurs before new ideas have been fully assimilated. For Vygotsky, peer interaction, collaboration and the involvement of more experienced others served to foster the cognitive conflict as new and challenging ideas were met.

Vygotsky's work is, however, generally differentiated from that of Piaget because of the increased emphasis that he places on culture and context. Vygotsky's theories also placed an emphasis on the role of language in thinking and in this his theoretical stance differs from that of Piaget. It has been suggested (Daniels et al., 2007: 3) that for Vygotsky "in order to comprehend the inner mental processes of human beings we have to step outside of the mind to look at these human beings in the sociocultural context".

Apprentices in learning

Vygotsky places a much stronger emphasis on the role of adults. His much-vaunted and widely misunderstood notion of a zone of proximal developmental (ZPD) is frequently referred to – probably giving it a much greater airing than Vygotsky intended. He was interested in the role of collaboration, particularly interactions with more experienced others (referred to in some texts as More Knowledgeable Others/ MKO) – who may be children or adults. Another beneficial feature of social relationships whether with children or adults for Vygotsky was the development of intersubjectivity – the development of shared meanings. Gray and MacBlain (2012) cite a study by Freund (1990) in which two groups of children aged between three and five years were given a task, which involved arranging furniture in a

———— Continued ➤

Profile (cont.)

doll's house. One group was given prior support from their mothers (which Gray and MacBlain interpret as offering ZPD). The other group was not given prior support (which Gray and MacBlain interpret as replicating Piaget's discovery learning). Unsurprisingly the first group outperformed the second.

Findings, such as these, need to be treated with care. Vygotsky himself identified play (which can be thought of as discovery learning) as offering children a zone of proximal development – allowing them to function at the very edge of their competence (1987). It is also important to consider what ZPD actually involves. The term *scaffolding* is widely credited to Bruner and it presents a useful metaphor through which to think about the way in which adults support children's learning. Effective scaffolding involves:

- a clear overall purpose (*intentionality*)
- *appropriateness* – problems which challenge children but which with help they will be able to complete
- *structure* – the use of questions and behaviours which children can imitate can support them
- *collaboration* – the role of the teacher is to build on children's attempts, to collaborate with them in the learning process. "The teacher's primary role is collaborative rather than evaluative" (Gray and MacBain, 2012: 81)
- *internalisation* – as children learn from their experiences, the adult's or more experienced other's support can gradually be withdrawn.

(based on Gray and MacBlain, 2012: 81)

Figure 5.1 Collaborative play

Continued ➤

Cultural tools

Another important feature of Vygotsky's theory is his use of the concept of cultural tools for learning. Culture is a vital element of Vygotsky's thinking and in his view all cultures have a set of tools which they use to support learning and thinking. Bruner (1986: 73) describes these as "a tool kit of concepts and ideas and theories that permit one to get to higher ground mentally… They provide a means for turning around upon one's thoughts, for seeing them in a new light."

Gray and MacBlain (2012: 73) suggest that "nursery rhymes, fairy stories, music and art" are all familiar cultural tools – so much so that we tend to forget their cognitive function. They cite Pea (1993, in Gray and MacBlain, 2012: 73) as saying that "these tools literally carry intelligence in them, in that they represent some individual's or some community's decision that [they should be] … made stable … for the use of others".

Transformations and multi-modalities

Vygotsky's work is characterised by the stress placed on the importance of transformations (Pahl, 1999). This is the notion that underpins much of the work at Reggio Emilia – representing ideas in one medium after another transforms the idea or concept. Gunther Kress (1997: 29) writes:

> the successive transitions from one mode of representation to another – from drawings; to coloured in, labelled drawing; to cut-out object; to the object integrated into a system of other objects, changing its potential of action; from one kind of realism to another; from one form of imaginative effort to another – these seem to me what humans do and need to do, and need to be encouraged to do as an entirely ordinary and necessary part of human development.

These transformations are reflected in the process of internalising ideas – concepts are formed and changed in the light of subsequent experiences or insights. Transformation is "a process that takes place in a complex series of shifts on the mind" (Pahl, 1999: 81). Vygotsky (1978: 56–7) writes about the process:

> firstly the external activity being understood internally, secondly the interpersonal process is transformed into an intrapersonal one, and finally the transformation occurs as a long series of developmental events.

Vygotsky is the first of the social constructivists. While he shared many of Piaget's views he opposed others. The theories of both have had a highly significant impact on current thinking about children's cognitive development. Nowhere is this more true than in thinking about the relationship between language and thought.

Key Debates

Language and thought

Viewpoint: Piaget believed that language is a system for representing the world but that it arises out of the stages towards logical thinking, which he advocated for other aspects of development. For Piaget, not until the end of the sensori-motor period, as symbolic representation begins to emerge, do young children start to use language and thought as representational systems in the way that adults do.

Sources: Cohen, D. (2002) *How the Child's Mind Develops.* Hove: Routledge (see Chapter 3).

Piaget, J. (2002) *The Language and Thought of the Child* [First published 1923. First English edition 1926]. London: Routledge.

Smidt, S. (2009) *Introducing Vygotsky.* London: Routledge (see Chapter 4).

Vygotsky, L. (1986) [First published 1934] *Thought and Language.* Cambridge, MA: MIT Press.

Counter viewpoint: Vygotsky believed that language supports the development of cognition, as Bruner (1986: 145) says of Vygotsky, he "assigns [language] a role as the nurse and tutor of thought". Vygotsky was influenced by the work of Charlotte Buhler (1893–1974), who later went on to become one of the leading figures in humanistic psychology (see Chapter 9). Buhler had studied the early development of language in babies and toddlers and believed that their early utterances were not symbolic but "social and emotional signals" (Cohen, 2002: 62) – a view also adopted by Vygotsky.

Vygotsky suggested that there were four distinct stages of development in the relationship between thinking and language. For him, a theoretical stance later taken up by Bruner, the stages are not one-way. Depending on the level of difficulty we may regress to an earlier stage. How often do you say things out loud to yourself when tackling something challenging or finding it hard to concentrate? The stages are described (Gray and MacBain, 2012; Smidt, 2009) thus:

- *The primitive stage* – at this stage speech is referential, object-oriented and social (Smidt, 2009). In other words it is used to communicate with others, and generally related to something in the here and now.
- *Practical intelligence* – at this stage language rules and structures come into play. Correct grammar begins to emerge and the vocabulary grows rapidly.
- *External symbolic stage* – the child begins to think aloud. This may be known as egocentric speech; inner speech or monologue. Vygotsky was clear that speech did not always require an audience. He also believed that egocentric speech occurred most frequently as children attempted "to master symbolic representation" (Cohen, 2002: 63).
- *Internalisation of symbolic tools* – by the age of seven or eight, thinking is generally internalised – except when thinking gets tough, and even adults may revert to the use of monologue! Thinking may still be guided by an inner voice but it is likely to be internalised. This allows for greater independence in cognition as it becomes a tool for thinking – to be used at will.

Continued ➤

While Piaget regarded egocentric speech as early speech that did not require a listener, Vygotsky carried out some experiments to find out something of its possible social function. He concluded from these experiments that:

- inner speech helped children to solve problems
- when speaking out loud, children expected to be understood and reduced the amount of utterances when it was clear that they were not being understood.

(based on Smidt, 2009: 65)

Experiments carried out after Vygotsky's death looked into the function of *acommunicative* speech, or language without any communicative intent. This might be thought of as language play, offering as it does practice, imitation, transformation and rehearsal – key elements of learning.

Post-Vygotskian social constructivists

Barbara Rogoff and Jerome Bruner are amongst the best known of the social constructivists but there are many others who emphasise tools for thinking and guided participation in particular. Kieran Egan (1991: 86) describes cultural tools appropriate to young children. He writes of the way in which:

> we recite proverbs, tell stories, teach rhymes, play verbal games, tell jokes ... to build the mental structures that systematize memory and poeticize the prosaic world, creating imaginative space and the power to be enchanted by magic and ecstasy.

Profile

Jerome Bruner

Bruner's work over many decades would enable him to be appropriately profiled in several chapters of this book. His early work was as a cognitive psychologist (see Chapter 8) focusing on perception – and seeking to discover what motivated the measured responses. This challenged the then contemporary focus on behaviourist interpretations of behaviour. He has also worked as a developmental psychologist. In some early work on language development (1983) he proposed a LASS (Language Acquisition Support System) in response to Chomsky's LAD (Language Acquisition Device) (see Chapter 3). For Bruner, LASS was a mother – challenging Chomsky's nativist theories and suggesting that nurture had some place in the development of learning. For Bruner (1986: 77) "it is LASS that helps the child navigate across the Zone of Proximal Development to full and conscious control of language use".

Continued ➤

Profile (cont.)

In the 1960s, he undertook a great deal of work on curriculum. It is in *The Process of Education* (Bruner, 1960: 33) that he famously proposed a "spiral curriculum" declaring that "any subject can be taught effectively in some intellectually honest form to any child at any stage of development". During the 1980s, Bruner worked on the Oxford Pre-School Research Project and produced some highly critical findings on the state of British early childhood education at that period. Kathy Sylva worked with him at that time – one of many highly illustrious collaborators, who have also included Howard Gardner and Margaret Donaldson.

He himself has been highly influenced by Piaget – recognising the importance of active learning, and by Vygotsky – placing great importance on the role of culture in shaping learning. In a chapter entitled *The Inspiration of Vygotsky*, Bruner (1986) cites him as having stated that "human learning presupposes a specific social nature and a process by which children grow into the intellectual life of those around them" (Vygotsky, 1978: 88). Bruner also believes that what he terms "*cultural psychology* is the route to understanding people's intentional behaviour" (Pound, 2005: 48). In his latter years he has also placed a strong emphasis on the role of culture in schooling (Bruner, 1996: ix – x):

> **What we resolve to do in school only makes sense when considered in the broadest context of what the society intends to accomplish through its educational investment in the young. How one conceives of education, we have finally come to recognize, is a function of how one conceives of culture and its aims, professed or otherwise ... culture shapes the mind ... It provides us with the toolkit by which we construct not only our worlds but our very conception of ourselves and our powers.**

In 1990, Bruner rejected the idea of the mind as a computer and focused again on Vygotskian ideas of culture and narrative. This shift from purely cognitive approaches towards aspects that make us human, that mark us out from computers was strengthened in 2003 with the publication of a book entitled *Making Stories: Law, Literature, Life*. Haven (2007: 10, citing Bruner, 2003) writes:

> **"stories create realities so compelling that they shape our experience not only of the world the fiction portrays but of the real world." [Bruner] is saying that the structure of story is so powerful that our minds automatically use story elements, story relationships, story architecture to understand and to make sense out of, the real-world events and people around us.**

Effective schooling

Viewpoint: Schooling around the world has a number of similar characteristics. It is usually compulsory. It generally involves large groups of children who are segregated both from all adults except the one or two allocated to the group of class and usually from children of any other age. Above all, schools are often segregated from real-life activities and motivations. Modes of teaching are often closely defined and teaching is broken down into small steps, which implies a continuing reliance on behaviourist theories.

Sources: Rogoff, B. (2002) *Learning Together: Children and Adults in a School Community.* Oxford: Oxford University Press.

Counter viewpoint: The work of a number of socio-cultural theorists challenges these assumptions. Their criticisms are not new. John Dewey was highly critical of the assumptions that underpinned statutory schooling. He believed that schooling should be part of life, not a preparation for it and that it should promote social progress. The role of the teacher was for him an active one – unlike the "negligible role" he believed many child-centred approaches demanded of adults. He described the role of the teacher as that of a leader within the social group of learners (Dewey, 1910). While Piaget regarded the environment as key to learning, Vygotsky highlighted the importance of the adult in engaging with children's current level of understanding and competence as a way of leading them on to the next stage. Many writers (see for example Cohen, 2002) suggest that this reflects Vygotsky's Marxist views that social situations are more conducive to learning.

Bruner and Bronfenbrenner have both picked up on the importance of socio-cultural contexts but in different ways. Bronfenbrenner's ecological system underlines the interconnectedness of the microsystem, mesosytem, exosystem and macrosystem as they surround the child (Darling, 2007). It is suggested that his theoretical approach has highlighted the importance of multi-professional working (Pound, in press) in practice to ensure that children's experiences and understandings are taken account of in supporting learning and development.

Bruner has over many decades attempted to put his socio-cultural ideas into practice. In 1965 he developed a curriculum "Man: a course of study" (Bruner, 1965), which he believed would address social and cultural issues by including communication; cultural tools such as media and the way in which societies organise around broad topics such as the arts, child-rearing and narrative. He highlighted in the curriculum framework what he regarded as alternative cultures such as Inuit and Kalahari bushmen. This attempt at putting his theories into practice now looks rather dated but what has impacted on practice is Bruner's theory of the development of cognition. He claims that ideas are represented through a series of modes, namely: the enactive, iconic and symbolic – which we all continue to use throughout life as we meet new ideas. This idea is widely seen in early childhood education where children are encouraged to enact or physically represent things through play, movement and physical action. The role of imitation in the process of learning is increasingly well understood (see for example Trevarthen, 2011).

Continued ➤

Key Debates (cont.) ?!

Rogoff (2002) challenges all the traditional assumptions about what makes for effective education. She suggests that effective education should be more firmly rooted in cultural systems. In order to achieve this she suggests the following foci:

- collaboration
- adult observation of children
- building on children's interests
- adults offering guided instruction (similar to Vygotsky's ZPD)
- opportunities to engage in cultural events with other members of the community – rather than always being segregated in age-specific groups.

Much of Rogoff's writing focuses on cultural tools for thinking. For her, like Vygotsky, the key tool is language, but mathematics is also an important cultural tool. Although hardwired in some way (Pound and Lee, 2010; Ramachandran and Blakeslee, 1999), in different societies there are many different cultural practices – abacuses, the use of fingers or other body parts for counting; or the disembedded practices of calculation or sums. On this subject Rogoff highlights some interesting research findings. Writing about the high mathematical achievement of Japanese children she suggests (2003: 265–6) that this is "surprising" given that:

> the emphasis in early childhood is on social development, not on instruction in academic subjects ... Japanese kindergarteners spend four times as much time in free play as in the United States, and Japanese elementary schools emphasize children supporting each other in learning together, not test scores. [It is] suggested that the Japanese children's impressive performance grows from the attention given ... to developing a sense of community in the classroom, so that the children feel a part of the group and are responsible to it, allowing a deeper and more focused attention to the subjects taught.

Profile

Urie Bronfenbrenner (1917–2005)

Bronfenbrenner is not usually seen as a social constructivist. However, the theory for which he is best known, ecological systems theory, relies heavily on socio-cultural views. He postulates four systems, representing them as four concentric circles. The first is called the *microsystem* – the child and those closest to him or her. Next comes the *mesosytem* – where all the links the "developing person"

Continued ➤

(as Bronfenbrenner describes the child) might meet occur. This might include the extended family, neighbours, nursery or place of worship. The third ring is labelled the *exosystem* – this is made up of people and places with which there is no direct contact but which might influence the child. This might be a parent's workplace or a sibling's school. Finally, the outer ring or *macrosystem* includes cross-cultural and broader influences or global similarities and inter-societal contrasts. Bronfenbrenner added a fifth dimension – not a circle but a time line – the *chronosystem* – perhaps best imagined as turning his set of circles into a cylindrical shape.

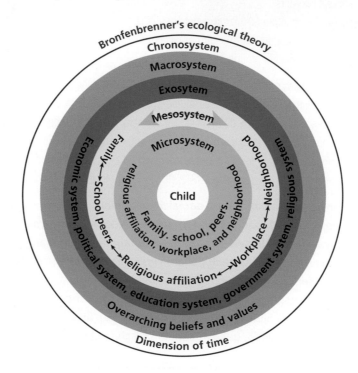

Figure 5.2 The ecological systems model (Bronfenbrenner, 1979)

Although not as widely known as others profiled in this chapter, Bronfenbrenner has made a significant contribution to thinking about learning and development. He was responsible for the setting up of Headstart programmes in the United States of America and in later life sought to explore how society makes human beings human (Bronfenbrenner, 2004). Before his death he made the rather gloomy prediction (2004: xxvii) that:

> The major social changes taking place in modern industrial society ... may
> have altered environmental conditions conducive to human development to

Continued ➤

Profile (cont.)

such a degree that the process of making human beings human is being placed in jeopardy.

Despite terming his theory an ecological one, Bronfenbrenner has been criticised for placing insufficient emphasis on the impact of nature on human development.

In Practice

Vygotsky himself sought to put his theories into practice. His role in supporting children with disabilities was to establish a system of education for "the pedagogically neglected" (Daniels et al., 2007: 3), the homeless and those with different cultural experiences. For him this meant developing "new ways to listen to and amplify the voices of the subjects who are marginalised, under-privileged, or in other ways silenced" (Daniels et al., 2007: 17) – an agenda which has a 21st-century ring to it.

Vygotsky's vision was of an active and involved teacher, seeking out and supporting every child's zone of proximal development; recognising learning as a social activity and understanding the necessary two-way interaction between the world of the classroom and the real world beyond its walls. In practice, ZPD is talked about a great deal, but not always fully understood. The sustained shared thinking discussed in the EPPE project (**http://eppe.ioe.ac.uk/eppe3-11/eppe3-11intro.htm**) has some resonance with Vygotsky's ideas. As the "guardian" of Vygotskian theory, Rogoff (1990, 2003) continues to support others in putting his ideas into practice, particularly with the notion of guided participation and an emphasis on the role of apprenticeship in learning.

Bruner's starting point has usually been a practical one as some of his areas of work demonstrate:
- the development of curricula (1960, 1996)
- evaluation of pre-school provision (1980)
- a practical theory for explaining the development of symbolic behaviour (1981), building on that of Piaget
- an explanation of scaffolding, building on Vygotsky's theory of ZPD (Wood et al.,1976).

Bronfenbrenner's contribution to practice is different. In focusing on the child at the centre, his work has been influential in enabling practitioners to understand the importance of working with parents and of multiprofessional approaches for early childhood care and education.

Research Methods

Many different research methods are used by the theorists described in this chapter. In much of the work you can see the historical links with philosophy. With Bruner, it is clear that his many interests will have led him to explore and reject a number of different research methods. The romantic view of Vygotsky, which arose from his early death and from the fact that his work was not published in the west until the 1970s, has meant that there has been little criticism of his work. But Cohen (2002: 70) reminds us that "Vygotsky's studies hardly conform to what are now considered good models of empirical practice. He hardly ever designed studies which attempted to falsify his hypotheses." Unlike Vygotsky, Rogoff, Bronfenbrenner and Bruner have all undertaken a great deal of research looking at a range of cultures and societies. In a lengthy discussion of research methods, Bronfenbrenner (1979: 20) rejects the idea that experimental methods are inappropriate to the study of human nature. In particular he rejects:

> the argument that because naturalistic observation preceded experimentation in both the physical and the biological sciences, this progression is necessarily the strategy of choice in the study of human behaviour and development ... In my view, twentieth-century science possesses research strategies that had they been available to the nineteenth-century naturalists, would have enabled them to leapfrog years of painstaking, exhaustive description in arriving at a formulation of biological principles and laws.

Next Steps

Pahl, K. (1999) *Transformations: Making Meaning in Nursery Education.* Stoke-on-Trent: Trentham Books.

Rogoff, B. (2003) *The Cultural Nature of Human Development.* Oxford: Oxford University Press.

Glossary

Acommunicative: without communication.

Cultural tools or tools for thinking: devices and artefacts devised and used within a culture for supporting learning.

Continued ➤

Glossary (cont.)

Ecological systems theory: comprised of the *microsystem*, the *mesosytem*, the *exosystem*, the *macrosystem* and the *chronosystem.*

Guided participation: Rogoff's preferred term for scaffolding or ZPD.

Intersubjectivity: shared meaning and attention.

Language Acquisition Device (LAD): Chomsky's hypothesis about the way in which language is learnt through hardwired mechanisms.

Language Acquisition Support System (LASS): Bruner's attempt to highlight the role of nurture in language learning. For him LASS = a mother.

More Knowledgeable Other (MKO): Older child or adult with experience, able to support a child's learning in the gap between what he or she can do alone and what can be done with support.

Multimodality: Perception that relies on two or more senses.

Scaffolding: see Guided participation.

Spiral curriculum: the learner returns to concepts, reshaping them with experience.

Zone of Proximal Development (ZPD): the distance between what a child can do with assistance and what the child can accomplish without assistance.

Summary

In undertaking an assignment on cognition you may like to consider making reference to some of the key issues explored in this chapter, including:

- theories with an emphasis on cultural considerations are not only constructivist – they may also encompass Bandura's social learning theory or Bronfenbrenner's ecological systems theory
- the role of adults is crucial in this theory, unlike Piaget's theories where it was much less clear. In social constructivist theories, adults offer scaffolding and guided participation and pass on cultural tools for thinking and learning
- socio-cultural theories do not on the whole discount inherited aspects of cognition (although Bronfenbrenner has been criticised for underplaying them).

Multiple Intelligences

Introduction

Howard Gardner claims to challenge the views of intelligence put forward by many other theorists. In 1983 he published the first edition of *Frames of Mind*, which challenges the whole notion of intelligence as a measurable entity. Gardner offers his Multiple Intelligence Theory (MIT), which has been highly influential in schools, particularly in the English-speaking world. Gardner has also collaborated with Reggio Children in his writing. In this chapter, MIT is explored and its applications and limitations examined.

This chapter covers aspects of the work of:
● Howard Gardner.

It also highlights key debates around:
● Is MIT reliable, consistent or credible?
● Is learning visible?

Profile

Howard Gardner

Howard Gardner was born in Pennsylvania but only discovered that he had had an elder brother when he found a newspaper cutting relating his death. This discovery, he claims (Gardner, 1989), gave him a strong sense of duty – a sense that in some way he needed to compensate his parents for the loss of their elder son. Gardner began his studies at Harvard University in 1961, and perhaps unusually in academic circles, has remained there ever since.

— Continued ➤

Profile (cont.)

Gardner relates the diverse influences that have shaped his thinking and theories. One of these influences was Erik Erikson, Gardner's tutor for a time. His influence on Gardner was threefold in emphasising the importance of observation in understanding learning; the impact of personality on learning; and a focus on developmental psychology (Gardner, 1989). Another major influence on Gardner's work has been the time that he spent working with Jerome Bruner (Gardner, 2001). In the course of his work with Bruner, Gardner learnt of Piaget's work and, through that of Levi-Strauss, the importance of cultural influences on learning. Again, perhaps unusually for an academic, Gardner has undertaken a number of related practical roles such as a teacher of young children and working with schizophrenic patients.

Multiple Intelligence Theories (MIT)

The intelligence tests developed by Binet (see Chapter 2) were widely regarded (Gardner, 2006b: 3) as "psychology's biggest success – a genuinely useful scientific tool". However, Gardner believed that intelligence is "too important to be left to intelligence testers" (1999: 3). He (2006b: 5) argues that intelligence testing reflects a one-dimensional view of intelligence (or "IQ or SAT mind") and as such cannot adequately describe the complex nature of the intelligences that human beings possess. He, on the other hand, claims to view intelligence as pluralistic, requiring supportive evidence from:

- *Brain research* – Gardner claims (1999) that neuropsychology has provided evidence of particular areas of the brain responsible for particular intelligences.
- *Human development* – different intelligences involve distinct developmental journeys.
- *Cross-cultural comparisons* – developmental journeys are shaped by the culture (Gardner, 1999: 39).
- *Evolution* – Gardner (1999: 36) suggests that evolutionary psychology has given new insights into the human brain and new tools for students of human cognition.
- *Identifiable core* (or *subintelligence*) operations – it seems likely that individual intelligences have a subset of capacities. For example, Gardner suggests that the subintelligences associated with spatial intelligence might be "sensitivity to large-scale, local, three-dimensional and two-dimensional spaces" (1999: 37).
- *Susceptibility to encoding within a symbol system* – such as spoken and written language, musical notations and mathematical systems of numerals and signs which have in Gardner's view arisen "to code those meanings to which the human intelligences are most sensitive" (1999: 37).
- *The existence of people displaying exceptional evidence of the intelligence (such as savants, prodigies, etc.)* – Gardner describes the impact on his theory of those with singular exceptional qualities such as those shown in the film *Rainman* – people who are, for example, able to identify which day of the week any date will fall on; or play a lengthy piece of music from memory after just one hearing.
- *Experimental psychological tasks* – discrete intelligences may be identified by asking subjects to do two things at once. If the tasks fit into different intelligences the subject will have no difficulty. Examples of this might include walking and talking. However, if the tasks call on the same intelligence, such as doing a crossword puzzle while paying attention to the words of a song, there will be interference and the subject is likely to have difficulty completing the task.

Continued ➤

- *Psychometric findings* – although intelligence test results do show some correlation between some aspects of measured intelligence (1999: 40), they vary in intensity. There are, for example, very weak correlations between linguistic and spatial intelligence. Goleman's work (1996) on emotional intelligence does not link to measures of linguistic or logical intelligence (Gardner, 1999: 41).

A number of intelligences have thus been defined. Initially, these were:

- musical intelligence
- bodily-kinaesthetic intelligence, which is to be found not just in dancers or gymnasts but in others such as craftspeople and surgeons
- logical-mathematical intelligence
- linguistic intelligence
- spatial intelligence, which is used by architects and chess players; pilots and sculptors
- interpersonal intelligence, which concerns contact with others, and
- intrapersonal intelligence, which concerns self-awareness.

Surgeons are mentioned by Gardner (1999) as needing both bodily-kinaesthetic and spatial intelligence and this highlights an important aspect of the theory. Musicians, for example, do not simply require musical intelligence – they also need high levels of interpersonal intelligence in order to stay in tune – literally and metaphorically with others. Novelists need not only linguistic intelligence but also intrapersonal intelligence.

After giving a lecture on MIT, Gardner reports that a member of the audience commented "you will never explain Charles Darwin with the set of intelligences that you proposed" (Gardner, 2006a: 18). This remark caused him to rethink his view, since Gardner has great respect for Darwin and has described him as having done "more than any other figure to stimulate scientific study of the mind" (1993a: 24). He then added *naturalist intelligence,* which enables some people to become expert at distinguishing "the diverse plants, animals, mountains, or cloud configurations in their ecological niche" (Gardner, 2006a: 19).

Similarly pressed to consider a spiritual intelligence, Gardner has concluded that spirituality is too closely associated with particular religions to qualify as an intelligence. Instead he has proposed an *existential intelligence* (or the intelligence of big questions). Gardner has also suggested that interpersonal and intrapersonal intelligences may be merged as a social intelligence or may simply underpin all other intelligences.

Key Debates

Is MIT reliable, consistent or credible?

Viewpoint: Gardner robustly challenges the notion of measurable intelligence at a fundamental level. More specifically, he claims to be "sceptical about the existence of horizontal features of cognition ... alleged to

Continued ➤

operate equivalently across all kinds of content" (2006b: 75). He regards horizontal features as equivalent to general intelligence (discussed in Chapter 2). Instead he argues that what other psychologists regard as general intelligence he regards as being specific to each of the multiple intelligences – and thus vertical features.

He further claims that all of the intelligences he identifies are of a similar status – objecting to the idea that some may be described as abilities while others are regarded as mere talents. Furthermore, he argues that intelligences, particularly those linked to mathematics and music, are largely inherited.

Sources: Claxton, G. (2008) *What's the Point of School?* Oxford: One World Publications.

Eysenck, M. and Keane, M. (2010) *Cognitive Psychology* (6th ed.). Hove: Psychology Press.

Gardner, H. (1999) *Intelligence Reframed.* New York: Basic Books (see Chapter 6).

Gardner, H. (2006b) *Multiple Intelligences: New Horizons.* New York: Basic Books (see Chapter 5).

Howe, M. (1999) *Genius Explained.* Cambridge: Cambridge University Press.

Counter viewpoint: Cognitive psychologists (see for example Eysenck and Keane, 2010) have suggested that all cognition is underpinned by attributes such as memory; perception; problem-solving and reasoning. Although Gardner (2006b) argues against what he terms "horizontal" capacities, he writes that, "much of the research in this tradition overlooks too many important aspects of human intellect" (1999: 87). It seems likely, for example, that the many types of memory listed by Gardner – immediate memory, short-term memory, long-term memory, semantic (or generic) memory, episodic memory (memory for particular events), procedural memory (knowing how) and propositional memory (knowing that) – are all required for all of his multiple intelligences. If we take dance as an example of bodily-kinaesthetic intelligence:

- immediate memory to support the guidance or decision just taken
- short-term memory to remember a dance sequence just agreed upon
- long-term memory to ensure an accurate performance
- generic memory to ensure that the full range of dance steps are known and remembered
- episodic memory to help ensure that the same mistakes are not made over and over
- knowing how to perform certain movements and knowing that a partner's sequence is followed by a different sequence

would all be part of a particular dance. Horizontal skills appear to apply equally to vertical intelligences.

The notion of vertical components must also be questioned on the basis of his criteria relating to evolution. Archaeologist, Steven Mithen (1996: 146) offers evidence that supports Gardner's view of domains in so far as "all Early Humans had multiple intelligences, each dedicated to a specific domain of behaviour" and agrees that these had "very little interaction between them". However, in the case of modern humans, our minds exhibit "cognitive fluidity" which allows ideas to move horizontally between domains.

Continued ➤

Theorists such as Claxton (2008a) highlight the role of learning abilities that underpin the whole curriculum such as critical thinking, empathy and imagination – presumably seen as horizontal or general abilities. Taking the example of logic, general intelligence or learning ability, Gardner (2006b) criticises mathematicians for arguing that knowing how to be logical means that logic can be applied in any situation. He adds that they often prove not to do this or to apply logic inappropriately. This is an interesting argument since:

- Logic is not unique to mathematics and they may be applying it inappropriately because of the way in which it has been taught. Inappropriate use of logic would appear to argue for horizontal rather than vertical application.
- Logic is not the only way in which to think mathematically (see for example Devlin, 2000) who argues that mathematical problem-solving requires intuition. Only when the mathematician has an intuitive answer does he or she begin to work out the logical proof.

Expert or talented?

While arguing that musical or bodily-kinaesthetic intelligences should not be viewed as mere talents, Gardner's viewpoint is at odds with studies of genius (see for example Howe, 1999). These indicate that the 10,000 hours required to become expert at anything can only be achieved through a willingness to or preference for spending that amount of time on a particular domain or interest. In turn, spending that amount of time will enable a person to become competent. In short, current debates about capacity tend to the view that it grows in relation to preference. Mozart's undoubted musical intelligence did not mean that he did not have "to put in the hours" (Pound and Harrison, 2003).

Figure 6.1 Becoming an expert by 'putting in the hours'

Continued ➤

Key Debates (cont.)

Indeed, research into the lives of professional musicians indicates that, contrary to popular belief and Gardner's assertion, their musicality was not usually inherited (see for example Sloboda and Davidson, 1996). However, their parents showed considerable interest in their children's musical activities and early experiences of music emphasised fun – both factors supporting the notion of enjoyment enabling enthusiasm and competence. Gardner does acknowledge, perhaps a little patronisingly, that "shrewd environmental interventions can convert ordinary people into highly proficient performers or experts" (1999: 88).

Additional criticisms

It is no surprise that a theory as challenging to existing ideas about intelligence should be widely criticised. There is a question mark over whether personal

Figure 6.2 Mozart (1756–91)

intelligences, in particular, can be readily symbolised within a symbol system. Other critics (see for example White, 2008; Klein, 1997) have raised additional issues. White (2008) suggests that MIT has arisen out of Gardner's personal history – the roles he has undertaken, the theorists with whom he has worked and so on. Given Gardner's references to his career (1999) this idea has credibility. Similarly, White argues that his theory has become too subjective or intuitive. Klein (1997) argues that in outlining his theory as strong, Gardner has exposed the gaps supporting his arguments. Publishing the weaker argument, which Klein suggests would be more appropriate, would render his theory less interesting.

In Practice

Despite the widespread criticisms, Gardner's work does have important strength and influence in practice. While acknowledging "the unevenness of the theory's application" within education, Kornhaber (2001: 276) suggests that its influence amongst teachers has occurred because it:

> validates educators' everyday experience; students think and learn
> in many different ways. It also provides educators with a conceptual
> framework for organizing and reflecting on curriculum, assessment and
> pedagogical practices. In turn, this reflection has led many educators to
> develop new approaches that might better meet the needs of the range
> of learners in their classrooms.

Continued ➤

Gardner (2006b: 23) himself identifies conclusions that point to practical applications. The first is that educators should start from the assumption that all children have the potential to achieve in all the intelligences that make us human. This does not mean that there are not individual differences but that we cannot predict who will be good at or especially interested in a particular domain or subject.

Second, Gardner's conclusions highlight the importance of individualised education, taking individual differences seriously. This requires careful assessment – not slavish testing of every child – but simply attempting to diagnose the nature of the difficulties when a child appears to be struggling. In addition, the child-led curriculum characteristic of Te Whariki, Reggio Emilia and Early Years Foundation Stage (EYFS) are in keeping with individualised curricula. Many of the practical applications of Gardner's work have been in secondary schools but there are some useful examples of its application to pedagogy in the early years.

Howard Gardner has taken a particular interest in the work of educators in Reggio Emilia. Within that approach, he stresses the value of collaborative learning; symbolic behaviours; the involvement of parents and community; and teaching methods built on discussion and on children's discoveries (Guidici et al., 2001). At Harvard University, Gardner has established a project known as Project Zero or Project Spectrum. Its aim has been to show that although every child has "a distinctive profile of different abilities, or multiple intelligences" these can be improved or developed through "an educational environment rich in stimulating materials and activities" (Chen et al., 1998: xiii). Gardner compares his work at Harvard with that in Reggio Emilia and concludes that:

- Project Zero grew out of theories while work in Reggio Emilia grew out of "promising practices" (Guidici and Krechevsky, 2001: 338).
- The employment of visual artists (or *atelierista*) in Reggio Emilia has led to an emphasis on visual forms of symbolic representation; while at Harvard the focus has been linguistic and musical intelligences and aural representations.

Key Debates

Is learning visible?

Viewpoint: Current policies on assessment in the early years are based, suggest practitioners in Reggio Emilia, on the assumption that learning is not visible.

Sources: Guidici, C. et al. (2001) *Making Learning Visible*. Reggio Emilia: Reggio Children.

Continued ➤

6

Key Debates (cont.)

Counter viewpoint: A group representing both Project Zero and Reggio Children collaborated on a project to explore the effectiveness of group learning (Guidici et al., 2001). The features or assumptions underpinning their work (Guidici et al., 2001: 18) were as follows:

- The members of learning groups include adults as well as children.
- Documenting children's learning processes helps to make learning visible and shapes the learning that takes place.
- Members of learning groups are engaged in the emotional and aesthetic as well as the intellectual dimensions of learning.
- The focus of learning in learning groups extends beyond the learning of individuals to create a collective body of knowledge.

Their joint project set out to demonstrate that through documentation of learning, formal assessment is rendered redundant. The editors write (Guidici et al., 2001: 22–3) that:

> Our research is based on the notions that theory can result from as well as contribute to classroom practice, and that documentation of learning processes is critical to the research enterprise ... By making individual and group learning visible [through documentation] we hope to contribute to the collective inquiry into teaching and learning and to the creation of ... "a culture of research".

Documentation in Reggio Emilia includes videos, tape recordings, written notes and evidence of the children's work – drawings, models and so on. It records the process of learning and is regarded as "visible listening" (Rinaldi, 2001: 83). It enables not only adults but children as individuals and as a group to observe learning. Its major advantages are (Rinaldi, 2001) that it supports groups and individuals in thinking about thinking (metacognition) and promotes re-cognition or reflective thinking about the learning situation. Moreover, it supports memory not only of the outcomes but of the processes involved in a particular experience or piece of learning. It is not that assessment is unnecessary but that formal assessments do not do the things that documentation make possible. Rinaldi (2001: 87) describes documentation as "the genesis of assessment" and makes it possible for the pedagogista to plan for further learning.

After this fruitful collaboration between Howard Gardner and his associates, and personnel from Reggio Children, it is puzzling to find a chapter written by one of the editors of *Making Learning Visible,* Mara Krechevsky (Krechevsky and Seidel, 1998), which outlines the tests used on Project Spectrum. The chapter seeks to draw a comparison between a child's reaction to a Stanford-Binet intelligence test and the battery of tests used on Project Spectrum. The strengths of both are outlined but the link with Reggio and its focus on assessing learning in action, rather than through tests, seems to have been lost or ignored in the American context.

Research Methods

Gardner highlights the two different meanings of the term 'theory'. He talks of the layperson's use of the term to describe a loose set of ideas. Physical scientists on the other hand, he describes as developing theories from "an explicit set of propositions linked conceptually and having individual and joint validity that can be assessed through systematic experimentation" (1999: 97). He goes on to suggest that, like many scientific theories, MIT falls somewhere in between these two extremes:

> There is no systematic set of propositions that could be voted up or down by a board of scientists, but the theory is not simply a set of notions I dreamed up one day. Rather I offer a definition, a set of criteria for what counts as an intelligence, data that speak to the plausibility of each individual intelligence, and methods for revising the formulation.

The methods for revising the theory are important but the fact that changes may occur as a result of new evidence does not demolish a whole theory. Piaget's overall theory of cognition has remained of interest despite many challenges to specific propositions. Simply because Margaret Donaldson has demonstrated contexts and conditions under which results of Piaget's test and experiments differ from those which Piaget found does not mean that his theory no longer has currency.

Gardner describes his wish to develop a set of fair tests for each of his intelligences. He outlines the difficulties posed by such a task and concludes that he discarded the idea since if he were to succeed he would be moving away from his original wish to avoid labelling or "the creation of a new set of 'losers'" (1999: 98). His view of intelligences is that they should support learning.

He describes some of his work with Project Spectrum where he is attempting to develop "intelligence-fair" measures amongst pre-school children. He suggests that any intelligence must only be assessed through the use of a variety of measures designed to reflect ability in subintelligences. For example, he suggests that an assessment of spatial intelligence would need to include measures such as finding one's way in unfamiliar territory, completing an abstract two-dimensional puzzle and creating a three-dimensional model of a known building.

The data that Gardner offers is drawn from research outlining findings from a range of disciplines including neuroscience, psychology and anthropology (1983). Since the publication of the first edition of *Frames of Mind*, there has been other research evidence which Gardner believes support his theory. Of particular interest is his view that the personal intelligences (interpersonal and intrapersonal) do seem to be indicating "that intelligence about the human sphere is independent from intelligence with respect to other realms of experience" (1999: 85).

Next Steps

Gardner, H. (2006b) *Multiple Intelligences: New Horizons.* New York: Basic Books.

(See Chapter 6 on nurturing intelligences in early childhood, which will give an insight into both research methods and the applications of MIT.)

Glossary

Bodily-kinaesthetic intelligence: refers to dance and movement as well as craftspeople and surgeons.

Episodic memory: memory for particular events.

Existential intelligence: concerned with the big philosophical questions of life.

Interpersonal intelligence: concerns contact with others.

Intrapersonal intelligence: concerns self-awareness.

Metacognition: thinking about thinking.

Naturalist intelligence: concerned with knowledge and awareness of nature.

Pedagogista: adult responsible for curriculum development in Reggio Emilia.

Procedural memory: knowing how.

Propositional memory: knowing that.

Semantic (or generic) memory: concept or knowledge-based memory.

Subintelligence: components making up an intelligence.

Summary

In undertaking an assignment on cognition you may like to consider making reference to some of the key issues explored in this chapter, including:

- the changing and sometimes analogous views put forward by Gardner – perhaps unsurprising since the first version of MIT was published 30 years ago
- the widespread interest in MIT and efforts to put it into practice
- the fact MIT arose out of dissatisfaction with intelligence testing and yet Project Spectrum appears to perpetuate their influence – albeit in the guise of offering something better.

7

Cognitive Psychology

Introduction

Eysenck and Keane (2010: 2) refer to cognitive psychology as including "four main approaches to human cognition", adding that "researchers increasingly combine two or even more of these approaches". Of these, issues associated with cognitive neuroscience and cognitive neuropsychology will be explored in Chapter 8. Elements of the remaining two approaches – experimental cognitive psychology and computational cognitive science – will be explored within this chapter. There is a confusing plethora and overlap of terms but the overall focus of the chapter will be cognitive psychology. Links will be made with what are widely described as *cognitive developmental* theories (see for example Keenan and Evans, 2010), which may include elements of Piagetian constructivist theories, Vygotskian socio-cultural or social constructivist theories as well as information processing theories. Perhaps by the end of the chapter the web of tangled terms will be a little clearer.

This chapter covers aspects of the work of:
● Ulric Neisser.

It also highlights key debates around:
● The brain as computer
● Of one mind?

What do we mean by cognitive psychology?

The period following the Second World War up to the mid-1960s (1945–65) is widely described as the period of the *cognitive revolution*. Miller (2003: 141) suggests that:

> Cognitive science is a child of the 1950s, the product of a time when psychology, anthropology and linguistics were redefining themselves and computer science and neuroscience as disciplines were coming into existence. Psychology could not participate in the cognitive revolution until it had freed itself from behaviorism, thus restoring cognition to scientific respectability.

Gopnik et al. (1999: vii), enthusiastic about the potential applications of cognitive science, describe it as a new discipline which "has united psychology, philosophy, linguistics, computer science and neuroscience". While psychology, as a discipline, had itself emerged from philosophy and physiology in the 19th century, in the mid-20th century cognitive psychology grew out of three major developments within mainstream psychology:

- A dissatisfaction with behaviourism which resolutely failed to look beyond actions, ignoring what was happening in the brain. Baars (1986) refers to this move as a revival of *cognitive psychology* since many early psychologists and philosophers had been primarily interested in the mind and its workings.
- The use of computer models to explain human behaviour, known as *cognitive science* (Johnson-Laird and Wason, 1977).
- The use of computer programs to reproduce human thinking, known as *artificial intelligence* (Fleck, 1982).

Profile

Ulric Neisser (1928–2012)

Neisser was born in Germany but emigrated with his family to the United States of America in 1933. His studies at Harvard University began in physics but he switched to psychology. At that time there were two main areas of psychological study – both had arisen in part as a rejection of introspective psychology, the starting point in the 19th century for psychology as a discipline in its own right. Introspection had been concerned with cognition in areas such as attention and perception. The method employed was that "highly trained observers reported on the activities of their own conscious minds" (Neisser, 1976: 2). By the 1930s the method had been abandoned, and psychologists became interested in "motivation, emotion and action" (Neisser, 1976: 2). Neisser claims that introspection was abandoned because it lacked *ecological validity* – that is to say that it had no application in the real lives of real people.

The two areas of study that had replaced introspection were:

- psychoanalysis with its focus on internal motivations driven by the libido, founded by Freud, and often known as "the talking cure", using language as a mirror on the mind; and
- behaviourism with its focus on actions rather than thoughts, led in the United States of America by Watson, followed by Skinner. It is sometimes said that at its most extreme, behaviourism rejects the existence of the mind.

This had resulted, claims Neisser (1976: 5), in "the public image of psychology ... that it dealt chiefly with sex, adjustment and behavloral control". Neisser believed that this had led to the neglect of cognition – with

——————————————————————————————— Continued ➤

little interest in how humans come to know and understand. Perception, which he describes as "the most fundamental cognitive act" (Neisser, 1976: 4), was studied by *Gestaltists*; and Piaget was working on *epistemology* (or the nature of knowledge) at the time. However, cognitive development, Neisser asserts, was largely ignored. This reveals the gap between the work of cognitive psychologists engaged in research and practitioners in the field of early childhood since, by the 1960s, Piaget's work was already widely known and valued by many of those working with young children. It may also reveal the gap between European and American psychologists.

In 1967, Neisser published a book entitled *Cognitive Psychology*. He is widely regarded as the key figure in the birth of cognitive psychology; "who helped lead a postwar revolution in the study of the human mind by advancing the understanding of mental processes like perception and memory" (Martin, 2012). In fact, "he even named the new field with the title of his 1967 book" which "set forth ideas advanced by him and other scientists that internal mental processes not only mattered, but could also be studied and measured" (Martin, 2012). His work was supported and strengthened by developments in computers and experimental techniques during the second half of the 20th century. This first book (Neisser, 1967) included a section on visual cognition, one on auditory cognition and a nod to what he termed higher mental processes – memory and thought.

In 1976, Neisser published *Cognition and Reality* in which he outlines the growth of interest in cognition – highlighting enhanced interest in Piaget's work and the publication of several journals on the subject of cognitive psychology. In this book, he places the emphasis on perception – a faculty he describes as "the basic cognitive activity out of which all others must emerge ... where cognition and reality meet" (1976: 9). Arguing that this is insufficiently well understood, even amongst cognitive psychologists, he continues (1976: 9):

> The prevailing view of [perception] tends to glorify the perceiver, who is said to process, transform, record, assimilate, or generally give shape to what would otherwise be a meaningless chaos. This cannot be right; perception, like evolution, is surely a matter of discovering what the environment is really like and adapting to it.

He highlights (1976: 5–6) the way in which:

> the computer itself seemed in some ways akin to cognitive processes. Computers accept information, manipulate symbols, store items in "memory" and retrieve them again, classify inputs, recognize patterns and so on. Whether they do these things just like people was less important than that they do them at all. The coming of the computer provided

Continued ➤

Profile (cont.)

a much-needed reassurance that cognitive processes were real; that they could be studied and perhaps understood. It also provided a new vocabulary and a new set of concepts for dealing with cognition; terms like information, input, processing, coding, and subroutines soon became commonplace.

However, Neisser's main aim in his 1976 publication was to demonstrate a need for changes in cognitive psychology. He criticises:

- the over-reliance on laboratory experiments, being he suggests over-used because experiments are more manageable. A focus on manageability undermines the ecological validity of the researchers' findings by ignoring the everyday contexts and roles in which people find themselves.
- researchers' failure to pay proper attention to real-life situations. He suggests that they "may have been lavishing too much effort on hypothetical models of the mind and not enough on analyzing the environment that the mind has been shaped to meet" (Neisser, 1976: 8).
- the poor quality of tasks that in no way match up to the sophisticated and complex cognition of which human beings are capable
- cognitive psychologists' failure to consider the true meaning of their work, adding that "human nature is too important to be left to the behaviorists and psychoanalysts" (Neisser, 1976: 8).

This underlines Neisser's willingness to review his ideas, and make changes. He praises the work of Jean Piaget who is sometimes described as a cognitive developmental theorist (see for example Keenan and Evans, 2010); and of Tom Bower, a developmental psychologist who pioneered work in investigating the perceptual world of infants, including neonates (see for example Bower, 1982).

Key Debates

The brain as computer

Viewpoint: The metaphor of the brain as computer is widely used. The similarities between brains and computers are widely listed – both are believed to encode information that comes into the system and to transform it into output that can be used. Both have limitations of memory, both can manipulate symbols. Artificial intelligence and cognitive science research is based entirely on this analogy. Gopnik et al. (1999: 21) describe this comparison as "the conceptual breakthrough of the last thirty years of psychology" and as "the basis of the new field of cognitive science". In addition, computers can enable cognitive scientists to try out their ideas about how the brain works (Keenan and Evans, 2010).

Continued ➤

Sources: Cohen, D. (2002) *How the Child's Mind Develops.* Hove: Routledge (pages 25–8).

Gopnik et al. (1999) *How Babies Think.* London: Weidenfeld and Nicolson.

Keenan, T. and Evans, S. (2010) *An Introduction to Child Development* (2nd ed.). London: Sage (pages 45–9).

Counter viewpoint: Attractive as it may seem, there are a number of objections to this view. As enthusiastic as they are about the brain as a computer, Gopnik et al. (1999: 21) admit that "we don't know just what kind of computer the brain is" and that "it's very different from any of the actual computers we have now". They describe the way in which computer programs are developed by taking in data or information and translating the input into a string of symbols which are rearranged in such a way as to form what are termed, by cognitive scientists, "representations". However, the analogy is not entirely helpful since as Gopnik et al. (1999: 148) go on to say:

> Children don't have just a single, fixed program that goes from input to output. Instead, they seem to switch spontaneously from using one program to another, more powerful program. That makes babies and children look very different from the computers we have now.

Cohen (2002) cites arguments that suggest that our brains are *unlike* computers for contrasting reasons:
- Computers are designed whereas our brains have evolved, perhaps leaving intact obsolete elements which may mean that our brains are inflexible; or
- Since learning and socialisation are "the key processes in life", "our biology is infinitely adaptable" (Cohen, 2002: 27, citing Tooby and Cosmides, 1998).

Cohen (2002: 27–8) continues:

> In the course of evolution, human beings needed to recognise objects, outwit predators, identify plant foods, select mates, make tools, balance when walking, avoid snake bites, devise the most effective hunt-a-gazelle tactics and learn how to barbecue fish with a nice touch of herbs and many other skills. Tooby and Cosmides see each of these activities as a domain and each set of skills that allow such a set of behaviours as "domain specific".

Costall (2004) argues that theories of artificial intelligence are only viewed as successful because they overlook the really difficult issues which intelligent systems such as the human brain are able to solve. He compares the constructivist approach of Piaget with the nativist approach of Gibson – whom he claims believes that the structures that surround the child do not need to be constructed because they already exist. Despite their

Continued ➤

differences Costall sees both Piaget and Gibson as having in common an understanding that cognition and perception need to be rooted in the real world. Costall (2004: 85) writes:

> Contrary to the dominant approaches within cognitive psychology and artificial intelligence, [Piaget and Gibson] did not take our capacities for representation and symbolism for granted, but saw clearly that representational activities need to be grounded in our interactions with our surroundings.

Citing Brooks (1991), Costall continues:

> Typically artificial intelligence [AI] "succeeds" by defining the parts of the problem that are unsolved as not AI. The principal mechanism for this partitioning is abstraction. Its application is usually considered part of good science, not, as it is in fact used in AI as a mechanism for self-delusion. In AI abstraction is usually used to factor out all aspects of perception and motor skills ... [Yet] these are the *hard* problems solved by intelligent systems.

There is a danger in using an inanimate metaphor for the brain since it may dehumanise our view of people. As we saw in Chapter 5, early in his career Bruner had described himself as a cognitive psychologist. By the 1990s he was rejecting a view of cognition that linked thinking to computers and reverted to what he termed "cultural psychology". Gardner et al. (1996) and more recently Greenfield (2009) question whether computers, artificial intelligences, are in fact changing our brains. Greenfield argues that until we know more about how brains are being changed we should move cautiously. Supporters of the metaphor, like Gopnik et al. (1999), counter that our brains have always changed and evolved – they are computers that constantly rewire themselves. This is not a new argument. Gardner et al. (1996: 192) record the words of Plato. Countering the argument that the creation of writing would make people wiser, he reports Thamus as saying that, on the contrary, "this discovery of yours will create forgetfulness in the learners' souls, because they will not use their memories, they will trust to the external written characters and not remember of themselves".

A related area of concern involves choice and freedom. As we saw in Chapter 3, Skinner believed that human behaviour could be controlled through behaviourism. His work on teaching machines translated easily into work with computers because it was a very straightforward model. Neisser (1976) argues that knowing more about psychology, even cognitive psychology, does not make us more able to control others. More recent writing (Kahneman, 2011) challenges this by suggesting that industry and commerce are using the findings of cognitive psychology very successfully to control human behaviour. Kahneman (2011) outlines the way in which he believes we make choices and decisions and how we are influenced, almost unwittingly, in a number of ways.

Research Methods

Gopnik et al. (1999: 20) assert that interest in children's cognitive development was restored in the late 1960s by three factors. One was the growth of feminism, which enabled more women academics to enter universities. The second factor was the development of video cameras and audio tape recorders – both of which enabled closer study of children and babies. Piaget (and his wife) were able to record their children's reactions and actions in detail but as Gopnik et al. (1999: 21) remark, this technology enabled science to advance, providing research methods "that allow us ordinary idiots to do the same things as the astonishing geniuses" (like the Piagets). The third factor was the development of computer technology – a new analogy, which allowed people to think in new innovative ways about how the brain might work. These last two things together allowed cognitive scientists to "use camcorders to see children in a new way, and we could use the metaphor of computers to understand them in a new way" (Gopnik et al., 1999: 22).

Research methods in cognitive psychology don't however stop there. Developmental psychologists, like Tom Bower, were able to devise materials that allowed them to test out abilities and perceptions in new ways. Bower, for example, designed and used an ultrasonic sonar helmet which allowed young blind children to learn move freely (Bower, 1977a) – replacing visual perception with auditory perception. He also developed switching mechanisms, which gave insight into the motives and intentions of very young babies.

His interest in children's perceptions led him to some valuable insights on perception, an important part of cognitive psychology. Note his reference to Piaget's experimental work (Bower, 1977b: 84):

> Perception becomes less and less important as we grow. The information provided by our senses stays relatively constant throughout development. The way we interpret it changes.... While we adults suffer, or enjoy, the illusions that a conjuror produces, we know perfectly well that what we are seeing are illusions and that reality is different. The baby is affected by disappearance transitions in the same way, but he does not know that reality is different. This is something he has to learn ... [Similarly] try looking at a full bottle of some soft drink, along with the same amount of liquid in a glass. It looks as if there is far more in the bottle than in the glass. Nonetheless we accept that the amounts are the same if we have seen the contents of them poured into the glass. A child under six doesn't accept this. For him there is less in the glass than in the bottle. He allows the evidence of his senses to dominate his judgement.

Continued ➤

Research Methods (cont.)

The emphasis in cognitive psychology has traditionally been on laboratory-based experiments and this has brought some criticism since it means that findings may have less ecological validity, a view dismissed by Bronfenbrenner (1979) (see Chapter 5). It has, however, meant that a range of technological devices have been developed and used. Many experiments with babies for example use "length of gaze" as a measure of babies' responses. Machines which show a stimulus for a very short measured time-span are also used. Neisser (1976) reminds us that these experiments disconnected from reality must be brought together with everyday understandings if they are to have genuine meaning.

In Practice

In bringing perception and other unseen aspects of cognition to the forefront of thinking and research, cognitive psychology has placed psychology in a position where it is seen as having a much wider application than simply "sex, adjustment and behavioural control". In the 2010 edition of their book, Eysenck and Keane include visual perception, memory, thinking, attention, language, reasoning, judgement, decision-making, problem-solving, emotion and consciousness. This vast array of topics has applications in every field of modern life. Kahneman (2011) shows the application of findings in these areas in politics, economics, advertising, medicine – in fact in virtually every aspect of both personal and professional lives.

Meltzoff (2004) identifies a number of areas of experimental cognitive psychology, which are impacting on practice. He suggests that the Piagetian viewpoint that representation only emerges at around 18 months of age has been undermined by evidence that babies can and do imitate faces from birth and engage in deferred imitation of actions early in life. He makes similarly challenging claims for joint visual attention, highlights research that shows understanding of an adult's intention from about 15 months of age, and challenges the Piagetian view of object permanence.

The major factor in all of these and other similar studies is that they increase the view of the young child as intentional, purposeful and socially responsive. This increased respect for what very young children can do has impacted on practice by indicating that young babies are not blobs but are active, curious and competent beings. No one has done more than Colwyn Trevarthen to underline this social competence. Trevarthen has a strong interest in enabling parents, teachers and clinicians to support children's development. For example, he collaborated with Helen Marwick in writing a review of all relevant research findings in order to support evidence-based practice with children up to three years of age (Trevarthen and Marwick, 2002). More recent interest in the way in which music supports communication (see Malloch and Trevarthen, 2009) has also led him to promote the use of music therapy (Pound, 2009).

?!

Of one mind?

Viewpoint: Work on artificial intelligence and notions of the brain as a computer have led to the conclusion that only logical thought is of real value. Piaget's insistence on the primacy of logical thought is also widely supported.

Sources: Claxton, G. (1997) *Hare Brain: Tortoise Mind.* London: Fourth Estate.

Kahneman, D. (2011) *Thinking Fast and Slow.* London: Allen Lane.

Counter viewpoint: As we saw in Chapter 6, Howard Gardner rejects Piaget's view of human thinking. He suggests that Piaget's focus is on what Gardner describes as logical-mathematical intelligence, which includes "time, space, number and causality" (Gardner, 1993a: 20). He further asserts that in doing so Piaget ignores other forms of thinking such as those required by artists, athletes or politicians, for example.

Guy Claxton (1997) also argues for other "ways of knowing" and rejects our contemporary emphasis on what he terms "d-mode" (or deliberation mode) thinking. Claxton identifies three brain-processing speeds. The first is the kind of thinking that is "unselfconscious, instantaneous reaction" (Claxton, 1997: 1) – the kind of thinking that is needed when we don't have time to decide what to do next. The second is d-mode – thinking that relies on reason, logic and conscious thought. This is the kind of thinking that is needed for exams, for argument and negotiation. The third type Claxton describes as what we use to ruminate, contemplate or mull things over and in his view this essential aspect of cognition is constrained by d-mode. The speed of d-mode thinking prevents the brain from considering all possibilities and makes it rely on known solutions – jumping to conclusions, rather than using intuition. Paradoxically, the slow ways of knowing that he identifies may turn out to be faster in the long run. He writes (Claxton,1997: 4) that:

> It is only recently … that scientists have started to explore the slower, less deliberate ways of knowing directly. The newly formed hybrid discipline of "cognitive science", an alliance of neuro-science, philosophy, artificial intelligence and experimental psychology, is revealing that the unconscious realms of the human mind will successfully accomplish a number of unusual, interesting and important tasks if they are given the time.

Jerry Fodor, a cognitive scientist and psycho-linguist, published a book entitled *The Modularity of Mind* in 1983, the year in which Gardner first published his multiple intelligence theory. Fodor argues that the brain has two distinct systems (not to be confused with the two halves of the brain). The first he identifies as perception – or an input system (which includes language, hearing, sight and so on). The second, central system, he identifies as cognition. Mithen (1996: 38–9) describes the two systems:

Continued ➤

Key Debates (cont.)

?!

According to Fodor, input systems are encapsulated, mandatory, fast operating and hard wired. He calls them stupid. As such they contrast with cognition, the smart central system. Fodor argues that we know almost nothing about how the central systems work, other than that ... they operate slowly [and are] ... holistic.

In addition, the central system (Fodor, 1983) is creative and relies on analogy or metaphor. He regards this two-part brain as perfect for survival: "Nature has contrived to have it both ways ... to get the best out of fast dumb systems and slow contemplative ones, by simply refusing to choose between them" (Mithen, 1996: 39, quoting a conversation with Fodor).

Kahneman, like Claxton, regards intuition as a higher order thinking skill but proposes a rather different view, highlighting two cognitive systems. He suggests that most of what you do originates in what he terms system 1 but that system 2 takes over when things get difficult.

- System 1 operates automatically and quickly with little or no effort and no sense of voluntary control. It cannot be turned off and generates suggestions (intuitions, impressions, feelings, etc) for System 2. It relies on System 2 in detailed or problematic situations.
- System 2 allocates attention to the effortful mental activities that demand it, including complex computations but is usually in low-effort mode. The operations of System 2 are often associated with the subjective experience of agency, choice, and concentration. It may act on and believe in the suggestions of System 1.

(based on Kahneman, 2011: 21–2, 25)

Next Steps

Meltzoff, A. (2004) The Case for Developmental Cognitive Science: Theories of People and Things, in G. Bremner and A. Slater (eds) *Theories of Infant Development*. Oxford: Blackwell Publishing Ltd.

Mithen, S. (1996) *The Prehistory of the Mind*. London: Thames and Hudson (Chapter 3).

Glossary

Cognitive developmental theories: which may include Piagetian constructivist theories, Vygotskian socio-cultural or social constructivist theories as well as information processing theories.

Cognitive neuropsychology: cognitive neuropsychology is a branch of cognitive psychology that aims to understand how the structure and function of the brain.

Computational cognitive science: descriptions of cognition in computer algorithms and programs, based on computer science.

Experimental cognitive psychology: an approach to studying the brain based on laboratory-based experiments.

Neuroscience: any of the sciences, such as neurochemistry, that deal with the structure or function of the nervous system and brain.

Summary

In undertaking an assignment on cognition you may like to consider making reference to some of the key issues explored in this chapter, including:
- the wide range of research methods used in cognitive psychology
- the impact of technology on the development of cognitive psychology
- the arguments surrounding the idea that human behaviour can be characterised as or compared with a computer.

Neuroscience

Introduction

"The more we know about the brain, the more we realise how little we know about how our ability to think develops" (Cohen, 2002: 9). Neuroscientist Lise Eliot (1999: 192–3) agrees. She argues that "cognitive development is ... the growth of intelligence" and that "intelligence is notoriously hard to define". Neuroscience is often regarded as one aspect of cognitive psychology but it is also seen as just one tool in the study of the brain – not all neuroscientists are psychologists, neither are all interested in child development. There are many debates surrounding neuroscientific findings, some of which will be explored in the chapter.

This chapter covers aspects of the work of:
● Susan Greenfield
● Vilayanur Ramachandran.

It also highlights key debates around:
● Sensitive or critical periods in development
● Neuroscience and early education.

The development of the brain

If the physiology of the brain is not familiar to you, Eliot's book, *Early Intelligence* (1999) will provide a highly readable overview. On her theme of linking cognition to intelligence, Eliot suggests that head size has been used as a means of measuring intelligence. However, although there is some correlation between the size of the brain and measured intelligence (or IQ), the size of the brain cannot be directly linked to skull measurements since the thickness of the skull may vary significantly.

Another measure Eliot explores is the speed of reaction. Some tests use inspection time variations – that is to say they present a particular stimulus for a very limited time. Throughout childhood – up to approximately 15 years of age – children continue to increase their speed of response. Between birth and adolescence, Eliot estimates, the speed of neural processing of information will increase 16-fold. This increased speed is linked to an increased efficiency. Those with higher IQs burn less energy and work less hard than people with lower IQs, when performing the same task.

Eliot also draws attention to the role and development of the frontal lobes of the brain. The prefrontal cortex is responsible for higher order cognitive activities such as "attention, memory, language, creativity, planning and self-awareness" (Eliot, 1999: 404). She suggests that these areas, if damaged, have no effect on IQ since they are responsible for what Eliot terms "wisdom" (the term Claxton applies to his slow ways of knowing. See Chapter 7). The frontal lobes are the slowest part of the brain to mature and this means that children (in whom the frontal lobes are by definition not fully developed) are likely to have a poor sense of time, short attention span and a lack of self-control. Myelination, much of which occurs in infancy, is not completed until the mid-20s in the frontal lobes. This means that the fatty myelin sheath that covers the axons connecting neurons is not fully formed in that part of the brain and thus electrical transmission of information is impaired. The right hemisphere of the brain is larger and more developed at birth, giving the baby an emotional and motor advantage. By the age of two, the left hemisphere, linked to language and self-awareness begins to catch up.

Research Methods

Much of the research in this field has been undertaken, at least initially, with animals. For example, early evidence for critical periods for brain function came from studies of kittens. In a study by Blakemore (1982) one eye of a four-week-old kitten, with hitherto normal vision, was kept covered for just one day. This resulted in lasting damage to the visual cortex. The fact that animals are widely used in brain studies has led some theorists (see for example Bruer, 1999) to reject neuroscientific findings as being irrelevant to human development.

However, language studies cannot be carried out on animals and Annette Karmiloff-Smith, a well-respected professor of neurocognitive development, has highlighted a range of techniques used in research into language (Karmiloff and Karmiloff-Smith, 2001). Many of the techniques are used in other studies of cognition.

Brain imaging techniques

A number of brain imaging techniques are now available. You may see reference to:
- Magnetic Resonance Imaging (MRI), which uses the resonance of hydrogen atoms occurring in different densities in the brain, and gives a high-resolution computer-constructed image of neural tissues.

Continued ➤

Research Methods (cont.)

- Positron Emission Tomography (PET scan), which uses radiation that is generated as glucose is metabolised by the brain to map out the different areas of brain activity.
- Brain Electrical Activity Mapping (REAM), which is related to EEG (electroencephalogram), and records different electrical waves generated by the brain.

However, in general, only ERPs (event-related potentials) are used with babies and children. This technique is non-invasive. All that is required is to place "on the child's head a very lightweight hair net composed of sixty-four tiny damp sponges attached to sensors" (Karmiloff and Karmiloff-Smith, 2001: 40). The sensors record the electrical activity inside the brain as various tasks or activities are carried out. The advantage to researchers of this technique is that "ERP recordings generate information in real time about location and the timing of changing waves of brain activity" (Karmiloff and Karmiloff-Smith, 2001: 40).

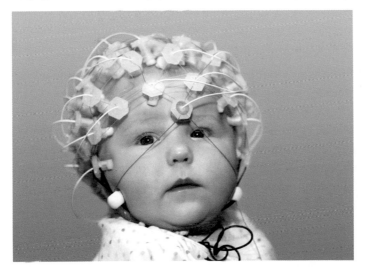

Figure 8.1 Non-invasive technique to record brain activity

While acknowledging the benefits of neuroimaging, Eysenck and Keane (2010) suggest that caution is needed since the long-term effects of the procedure are poorly understood and that problems of *ecological validity* remain. In other words, the tests and tasks applied are not real-life situations so researchers cannot be certain that the results obtained are what would be found in other situations. This is probably less true of work with young babies since everything is new and changing – as Bower suggested (1977, see Chapter 7) perception is more powerful in infancy than in later stages of development.

Neuroscientists take a fresh look at earlier studies

Eliot (1999) replicates a Piagetian experiment and offers an alternative interpretation. The task simply involves babies in retrieving an object (a bell in this example) hidden in one of two places directly in

Continued ➤

front of the baby. At eight months babies typically retrieve the object the first time (A), but if it is then hidden in the alternative place (B) the baby will look in the first hiding place. This happens despite the fact that the baby has watched the researcher 'hide' the object. Piaget's explanation was that the baby had not yet established object permanence. For a neuroscientist the explanation (Eliot, 1999: 409) is as follows:

> [the baby] remembers the bell's location in well B; she keeps her eye there even though her hand is reaching to the wrong spot. Her problem is keeping this information in mind while simultaneously blocking her impulse to reach back to well A. She can do it if the interval between hiding and retrieval is short enough, no more than two or three seconds, but keeping track of everything – remembering that the bell is in well B, that she has to remove a cloth in order to retrieve it, and that she must not reach to well A – for five full seconds is simply more than she can manage.

> "A not B" is harder than it seems; it requires planning, inhibition, working memory, and at least a minimal attention span – all frontal lobe functions that are still rudimentary in babies [of this] age. Each of these skills, however, will come to life over the next few months, as her frontal lobe kicks into action. By nine months, she can remember for as long as six seconds that the hiding place was switched, and by twelve months, she can remember it for a whopping ten seconds.

Profile

Susan Greenfield

Baroness Greenfield is a British scientist, writer, broadcaster, and member of the House of Lords. Greenfield's special area of interest is the physiology of the brain and she has a particular interest in Parkinson's disease and Alzheimer's disease. However, she is best known as a populariser of science – having written several popular-science books about the brain and consciousness, and regularly appearing on radio and television.

In a book entitled *Tomorrow's People*, she imagined a future world of "techno haves and techno have-nots" and has worked for the democratisation and increased accessibility of science in order to avoid such a future. Susan Greenfield, perhaps somewhat paradoxically, has expressed concerns that modern technology (see for example BBC, 2009; Derbyshire, 2009; Swain, 2011) may have a negative impact on child development.

Continued ➤

Profile (cont.)

In this respect, she has been criticised by Goldacre (2011). He suggests that as a respected scientist, Greenfield ought not to make such claims without providing formal evidence to support her arguments. According to Goldacre (2010), Greenfield has rebutted his criticisms by stating that is "like the people who denied that smoking caused cancer".

The insights of Susan Greenfield that:
- if we didn't move we wouldn't need a brain (1997), and
- play is fun with serious consequences (1996)

hold important implications for early childhood practitioners. The importance of movement in brain development is increasingly well understood (see for example Tobin, 2004; Walsh, 2004).

Profile

Vilayanur Ramachandran

Ramachandran was born in Tamil Nadu and was educated in India, Thailand and England. He gained a PhD at Trinity College Cambridge and is currently the Director of the Center for Brain and Cognition in San Diego, University of California, where he has been a professor since 1998. In 2011 he was named by *Time* Magazine as being among the most influential 100 people in the world **(www.time.com/time/specials/ packages/article/0,28804,2066367_2066369_2066125,00.html)**. He has been described as the "Marco Polo of neuroscience" and the "modern Paul Broca" – references to his brain studies.

His books and lectures on the subject of the brain are highly accessible and have served to publicise important aspects of neuroscience. (For an introduction to the brain you can watch a short video on **www.ted.com/talks/vilayanur_ramachandran_on_your_mind.html**.) He seems to have a particular gift – not just for explaining things in simple terms – but for developing conceptually simple experiments which get to the nub of an issue. His early work included, for example, helping patients to recover from pain in phantom limbs through the use of mirrors (Ramachandran and Blakeslee, 1999).

Of particular interest to early years practitioners are his explanations of theory of mind, the use of metaphor, and the role of mirror neurons. Theory of mind is linked to false belief studies (Cohen, 2002), and to mindsight (Siegel, 1999: 148), which enables us to "detect the emotional state of another". Describing theory of mind as "unique to humans" (Ramachandran, 2011: 118), he links it to work on mirror neurons, the discovery of which have transformed understandings of human empathy (Rizzolatti et el., 2006). For more detail watch Ramachandran's short video (**www.ted.com/talks/ vs_ramachandran_the_neurons_that_shaped_civilization.html**).

Continued ➤

Ramachandran (2011) identifies several functions of mirror neurons:

- to support imitation and learning
- to work out another's intentions
- to "adopt the other person's conceptual vantage point" reflected in phrases such as "I see what you mean"
- to develop self-awareness and the ability to think in the abstract.

Ramachandran believes that abstract thought is supported by our use of metaphor – a subject on which he has written widely. This links to Fodor's (1983) reference to our liking for analogy as a tool for cognition (see Chapter 7).

Key Debates

Critical or sensitive periods

Viewpoint: Bruer (1999) is particularly critical of claims about the importance of the first three years of life as critical to later brain development. The notion of sensitive periods has he claims been overstated because:

- The plasticity of the brain, together with the young child's resilience, means that the effects of early deprivation can be overcome and that damage to parts of the brain may be taken up by other areas.
- The emotive phrase "use it or lose it" refers to the pruning which occurs in the brain and implies that once pruned, abilities may be lost. Pruning can increase efficiency in the brain by simplifying or clustering networks of neurons (Eliot, 1999). The most dense arrangement of synapses for language occurs at three years of age, while for visual processing the density is greatest at around four months of age. The later pruning that occurs in these does not mean that language ability or visual perception are lost.

Sources: Blakemore, S-J and Frith, U. (2005) *The Learning Brain.* Oxford: Blackwell Publishing.

Bruer, J. (1999) *The Myth of the First Three Years.* New York: The Free Press.

Counter viewpoint: Blakemore and Frith (2005) argue that sensitive periods should not be seen as a disadvantage. Using the analogy of a self-closing window they suggest that sensitive or critical periods allow us to open new windows for learning while closing others which are less important. However, we also know that extreme deprivation at periods of development may be critical. Talay-Ongan for example argues that "prolonged periods of reduced linguistic input in early childhood affects the development of language" (1998: 52) and that "attachment, where the infant forms mental representations for his affection towards his mother or other primary carers in the first year of life, also seems such a time-dependent construct" (Talay-Ongan, 1998: 52). This view is strongly supported by Siegel (1999) who believes that attachment may be the only truly critical period – the only learning that cannot readily be replaced later.

Continued ➤

Key Debates (cont.)

Talay-Ongan highlights two other areas of deprivation, which may influence development adversely in irretrievable ways:

- Parental neglect, abuse, indifference or severe discipline seems to alter the circuitry of the prefrontal lobes of young children, affecting their emotional response style (1998: 52).
- Restriction of movement in the early years seems to prohibit the synaptic connections in the cerebellum. A child immobilised in a body cast until four years of age would learn to walk eventually but never smoothly (1998: 52).

Bruce (2011) describes sensitive periods in development when children may be able to learn things more effectively. She highlights the importance of Froebel's phrase that children should "at every stage be that stage" and writes:

> Froebel, Montessori and Steiner all believed that there are definite stages in development that require appropriate and sensitive handling. They all asserted that each stage is important in its own right and should not be accelerated, but enriched at that level instead.

She highlights children's schematic interests (see Chapter 4) as being an example of these sensitive periods – where children's interests may overwhelm other considerations and may be used as the starting point for learning. This tuning in to children and their enthusiasms is at the heart of learner-centred approaches to teaching.

Another area that deserves consideration in this debate is that of *resilience*. Gillian Pugh (2002) has highlighted the risk factors in children themselves, in families and in communities that are most likely to adversely affect development. Clearly many of these factors are ones that affect health and well-being in a variety of ways and are not necessarily the aspects of development referred to by Talay-Ongan as bound by critical periods. However, of interest is her description of resilient children. Citing Kraemer (1999), Pugh (2002: 110) argues that resilience is most easily acquired in babyhood and that it allows children to have the resilience "to get back in balance after being pushed out of it" and "to tolerate greater challenges without breaking down". It is of course worth noting that individual aspects of personality or temperament (which may or may not be genetic) can create wide variations in the development of resilience (see Gerhardt, 2004). It should also be noted that we cannot predict the resilience of individual children and must therefore work to protect all from harm.

In the revised Early Years Foundation Stage (DfE, 2012) three prime areas of development and learning have been identified: personal, social and emotional development; communication and language; and physical development. The rationale for privileging to these areas is that "if not securely in place between 3 and 5 years of age, they will be more difficult to acquire and their absence may hold the child back in other areas of learning" (Moylett and Stewart, 2012: 19). Although not a narrow window, the suggestion is that, in the eyes of the DfE at least, critical periods do exist.

Continued ➤

Neuroscience and early education

Viewpoint: Practitioners and parents are apt to privilege neuroscientifc findings (or brain research as it is often popularly known) over others – believing them to be more likely to be true than less biologically and technologically based evidence. Researchers such as Goswami (2004) and Willingham (2009) suggest that cognitive developmental neuroscience is having an impact on education in relation to milestones of development; work on dyslexia; and benefits to children with sensory or other developmental impairments or delay.

Sources: Bruer, J. (1999) *The Myth of the First Three Years.* New York: The Free Press.

MacNaughton, G. (2004) 'The Politics of Logic in Early Childhood Research: A Case of the Brain, Hard Facts, Trees and Rhizomes', *The Australian Educational Researcher,* 31, 3 December.

Counter viewpoint: John Bruer (1997) suggests that the field of neuroscience is too full of what he terms "neuromyths" to be of real value to educationalists. Willingham (2009) highlights three key reasons why neuroscience cannot answer all the questions that educationalists have. Characterising education as an "artificial science" and neuroscience as a "natural science", Willingham (2009: 544) argues that:

> *artificial sciences are driven by goals, and the desiderata set by some goals are ones for which natural sciences are not informative... Goals for children's education often include features to which the natural sciences will not contribute.*

Willingham's second line of argument is that neuroscientific research works outside the real world "for the sake of simplicity" (Willingham, 2009: 545) but teachers cannot. He gives the example of memory – neuroscientists and teachers know memory improves with repetition. However, within education this knowledge is constrained by recognition that too many demands for repetition will undermine motivation and thus hinder learning.

His third point is that much of the data collected by neuroscientists about the structure of the brain and the function of its parts is of no use to educationalists. He offers the following example: "suppose one concludes that the interparietal sulcus contributes to number sense in arithmetic. What's next?" (Willingham, 2009: 545).

MacNaughton (2004) suggests that early childhood specialists, keen for recognition, cling to what they see as hard data offered by neuroscientific findings in support of their work. However she rejects this idea – neuroscientific findings cannot provide answers that are sufficiently flexible, diverse or complex to represent the many variables of human beings. Claxton (2008a) adds a similar warning, arguing that neuroscience is in its infancy – that what we believe to be true today may well prove not to be so tomorrow.

Continued ➤

Key Debates (cont.) ?!

Enrichment

A number of animal studies have indicated the beneficial effects of enriched environments. Mice, for example, placed in environments offering rich opportunities for exploration and problem-solving developed cortical networks, denser than those raised in impoverished surroundings (Talay-Ongan, 1998). Innumerable examples from the field of early childhood care and education are based on the assumption that an enriched environment supports the development of effective learning and thinking. The pioneering work of Maria Montessori, Susan Isaacs and the McMillan sisters rested on just such a belief. Piaget's theories led practitioners to provide enabling environments. Chris Athey's work (1990) (see Chapter 4) pointed to an improvement in measured outcomes as a result of an enrichment programme of trips and visits. More recently the EPPE project (**http://eppe.ioe.ac.uk/eppe3-11/eppe3-11findings.htm**) and the longitudinal studies conducted by Weikart into the impact of HighScope (Schweinhart et al., 2005) have pointed to the impact of early intervention.

Blakemore and Frith (2005: 22–3) describe the process whereby:

> as soon as a baby is born, its brain connections start growing and changing. Which connections survive and grow and which fade away and die, is determined partly by the genes the baby inherits from its parents and partly by the baby's early experiences.

They then ask the question as to whether this process argues for enriched experience in infancy – to which they respond by drawing attention to the fact that the relevant studies have been done on animals and that animals have a shorter childhood than humans. This means that, "the period of rapid growth in brain development is in humans likely to be considerably longer" (Blakemore and Frith, 2005: 23). Any normal environment provides sufficient sensory input – problems only arise in deprived environments such as those found in the much-publicised Romanian orphanages. Hothousing is widely regarded as unnecessary, but some people believe it to be harmful – privileging as it does the mind over the body (Tobin, 2004). Blakemore and Frith (2005: 35–6) are more measured in their response:

> This is not to say that hothousing is necessarily damaging – it might be, but the necessary studies have not yet been carried out... [W]e sometimes hear warnings of not adding vitamins to our diet when it is not necessary... Similarly it is conceivable that the developing brain can be over-stimulated. What is not known is what the effects of such an overdose might be.

In Practice

As Willingham (2009) points out, not all neuroscientific findings have implications for practice and as McNaughton (2004) argues the implications of such findings have to be related to human factors. Neuroscience has, however, highlighted a number of factors, which may be applied in practice:

- Eliot (1999: 416) describes the brain of a six-year-old – "with a full-grown brain and a fully engaged frontal lobe, a six-year-old thinks much more like an adult than like the helpless newborn she so recently sprouted from. By this point, all the basic tools of cognition are in place". She asserts that "this is not a time for heavy academic instruction" (1999: 458) since children of five and under are not ready – emotionally or cognitively for the pressure and anxiety of more formal schooling.

- "Second-language learning is easiest in early childhood" (Talay-Ongan, 1998: 57). Babies are able to discriminate all speech sounds before six months and this capacity is gradually narrowed down to the sounds used in the languages to which a child is exposed. Gopnik et al. (1999: 192–3) write that:

  Children who learn a second language when they are very young, between three and seven years of age, perform like native speakers on various tests. If they learn after eight years old, their performance declines gradually but consistently, especially during puberty. If you learn a second language after puberty there is no longer any correlation between your age and your linguistic skill: twenty-year-olds do no better on the tests than forty-year-olds.

- "The vocabulary size of babies with highly conversant mothers is reported to be considerably larger than those with taciturn mothers, the gap being wider at 24 months than at 20 months" (Talay-Ongan, 1998: 53)

- "Right and left hemispheres can be prompted to work in tandem: music seems to excite the innate circuits, enhancing complex reasoning and maths skills" (Talay-Ongan, 1998: 57).

- "Emotional tonality set in infancy may assist in or hinder a child from self-regulating at later stages. It also seems to affect the ease with which the child adapts and interacts in a learning environment" (Talay-Ongan, 1998: 57).

- "Teaching young children to visualise as they listen to verbal material may enhance their comprehension of language" (Talay-Ongan, 1998: 57).

- "Interdisciplinary collaboration between neuroscientists, child development specialists and educators is an essential step towards uniting theory and practice with young children" (Talay-Ongan, 1998: 57). The field of developmental neuroscience holds much promise.

Continued ➤

In Practice (cont.)

- Mirror neurons should encourage practitioners to provide opportunities for imitation. In addition to the development of empathy, mirror neurons enable children to learn from the images of others they see undertaking movements.

Figure 8.2 Imitation plays an important role in learning

- Neuroscience holds some practical clues about supporting cognition. These include:
  - being born to a family with higher socio-economic status (Eliot, 1999)
  - being amongst the first-born in a family (Eliot, 1999)
  - prenatal care which protects children from low birth weight and avoids maternal stress (Pugh, 2002)
  - good nutrition and breast-feeding (Eliot, 1999)
  - opportunities for movement – floor time and outdoor time (Greenland, 2000; White, 2008)
  - recognition of the value of modelling and imitation – "it is the model we set rather than the specific teaching we attempt, that is going to have the biggest impact on a child's cognitive abilities and success in life" (Eliot,1999: 460).
  - responsive and involved adults – this does not mean smothering the child but tuning into their interests, sharing meanings and "being present" (Drummond and Jenkinson, 2009).

Next Steps

MacNaughton, G. (2004) "The Politics of Logic in Early Childhood Research: A Case of the Brain, Hard Facts, Trees and Rhizomes", *The Australian Educational Researcher,* 31, 3 December.

Willingham, D.T. (2009) "Three Problems in the Marriage of Neuroscience and Education", *Cortex,* 45 (4): 544–5.

Glossary

Ecological validity: For a research study to possess ecological validity, the methods, materials and setting of the study must approximate the real-life situation that is under investigation.

ERP (event-related potentials): A non-invasive technique for studying the brain in which a lightweight net composed of damp sponges attached to sensors is placed on the child's head.

Mimetic representation: using imitation to represent ideas of feelings.

Mirror (or empathy) neuron: a neuron that fires both when an animal acts and when the animal observes the same action performed by another.

Pruning: the process of weeding out unnecessary connections and strengthening the important ones, based on the child's experiences. Some pruning begins very early in development.

Resilience: refers to the idea of an individual's tendency to cope with stress and adversity. This coping may result in the individual "bouncing back" to a previous state of normal functioning, or simply not showing negative effects.

Summary

In undertaking an assignment on cognition you may like to consider making reference to some of the key issues explored in this chapter, including:
- this is a science in its infancy – its findings need to be carefully reflected on and separated from the high status in which they are held by many of the public
- a wide range of psychological approaches consider, and frequently embrace, neuroscientific findings
- the claims of neuroscientists offer many practical suggestions for education but MacNaughton's view that they may not yet have complete answers to the complexity of human nature should be heeded.

Cognition and Disposition

Introduction

In this chapter *the* key debate is whether or not our school system is achieving what it set out to achieve. The evidence for the impact that learning dispositions have on achievement is overwhelming. All around the world societies and cultures, families and communities want the best for their children – children *are* the future. But there are sharply differing views about how this can best be achieved. The more that is learnt about learning the more apparent it becomes that human learning is shaped, constrained or enhanced through the quality of social interactions, emotional factors and personal characteristics. Writers from many fields are sharing their belief that these qualities are what matter in education – but still views of what is relevant in schooling continue to be shaped by political expediency.

This chapter covers aspects of the work of:
- Carl Rogers
- Ferre Laevers
- Guy Claxton
- Daniel Goleman
- Carol Dweck.

It also highlights the key debate around:
- The purpose of schooling.

What do we mean by dispositions for learning?

There is a number of overlapping views about how best learning can be supported and developed through personal, social and emotional aspects of development, or in Gardner's (1999) terms the interpersonal and intrapersonal intelligences. Marion

Dowling (2010) reminds us that there is no clear consensus on what dispositions are the most important or desirable. She suggests that the ones most supportive of young children's learning and achievement are motivation, perseverance, curiosity, creativity, problem-solving and reflection.

Te Whariki

The five strands of Te Whariki, the New Zealand early years' curriculum framework, each have attributed related learning dispositions. These in turn are linked through the assessment tool, *learning stories* (Carr and Lee, 2012).

- To the strand of **belonging** is attributed *courage and curiosity,* assessed through taking an interest.
- To the strand of **well-being** is attributed *trust and playfulness,* assessed through being involved.
- To the strand of **exploration** is attributed *perseverance,* assessed through persisting with difficulty, challenge and uncertainty.
- To the strand of **communication** is attributed *confidence,* assessed through expressing a point of view or feeling.
- To the strand of **contribution** is attributed *responsibility*, assessed through taking responsibility.

Revised Early Years Foundation Stage

The revised framework (DfE, 2012) identifies characteristics of effective learning (2012:1.10). Stewart (2012) describes these as elements of self-regulated learning and highlights as key factors engagement, motivation and critical thinking. Stewart also adds to that list relationships and well-being, and then compares these elements to the characteristics of effective learning found in a range of curricular and theoretical approaches. This process highlights some important contributions to a positive learning disposition, including making connections, openness to failure, willingness to take risks, enjoyment and reflection.

Profile

Carl Rogers (1902–1987)

In the 1940s, Carl Rogers, along with Charlotte Buhler and Abraham Maslow, established what was termed a third force, humanistic psychology. Humanistic psychology was intended to offer a bridge between the then dominant fields of behaviourism and psychoanalytic theory. Humanism rejects behaviourism's denial of emotions and motives and believes that feelings cannot be ignored.

Continued ➤

Profile (cont.)

Psychoanalysts were seen as having too little respect for their clients – Freud, for example, frequently referred to the women who sought his help as "hysterics". Rogers developed an approach to psychoanalysis that has come to be known as "client-centred therapy". Its aim is to enable clients to become "fully functioning persons". This is akin to Maslow's term "self-actualisation".

The application of Rogerian therapy has been seen in many fields of work such as nursing and other caring professions. He himself recognised its importance in education, which is reflected in his book *Freedom to Learn*. In this book Rogers (1983; first published in 1969) uses a term which has become very familiar to early years' educators. He writes that as a relationship of trust developed between teacher and taught, his role shifted to that of a facilitator of learning (Rogers, 1983).

Rogers emphasises sense of excitement as a factor in supporting emotion and cognition – something which neuroscience supports. Eliot (1999), for example, describes the way in which excitement and enjoyment change the chemistry of the brain making learning more effective. Egan (1991) also refers to the importance of the ecstatic responses of young children. He also places stress on the value of child-initiated learning in order to ensure interest, involvement and understanding.

Profile

Ferre Laevers

Ferre Laevers began his work on experiential education in 1976, his aim being to discover more about what he terms "deep-level learning". He began his research with just 12 teachers but he now works with institutions and education departments in over 20 countries around the world.

The key for Laevers is the involvement of the child in learning, which he believes is characterised by concentration, energy, complexity, creativity, persistence, precision and a sense of satisfaction. He suggests that these can be gauged through observation of facial and verbal expression, and through the vitality or speed of response. He suggests that this level of involvement comes from a sense of well-being, an idea closely linked to the work of Carl Rogers and Abraham Maslow. The scales devised by Laevers to enable teachers and educators to screen for involvement and well-being cite the following key characteristics of well-being:

- Feeling at ease
- Spontaneity

Continued ➤

- Open to the world around
- A sense of inner relaxation
- Vitality and self-confidence
- Being in touch with one's own feelings – in short enjoying life.

In order to support learning, the role of the adult is seen as being engagement in and awareness of what children are doing and feeling. This will involve sensitivity, stimulation and promotion of independence and autonomy. Also essential is an enabling environment – that helps children to make connections between previous experiences and between peers, adults and the materials available to them. He reminds practitioners that activities which are not sufficiently challenging (such as colouring or tracing) are unlikely to encourage involvement in learning.

Profile

Guy Claxton

Guy Claxton is probably best known currently for his project Building Learning Power. His decades of writing and research challenge mainstream thinking about education. He has coined the phrase *learnacy*, as a counter to what he sees as the current over-emphasis on literacy and numeracy and lack of concern for learning in general. Claxton proposes four rather than the usual 3Rs: resilience, reflection, reciprocity and resourcefulness. These he explains involve respectively:

- Sticking at things
- Taking stock of your own learning
- Being able to work alone and with others
- Being able to learn in different ways.

Among the most interesting aspects of Claxton's work are his emphases on the role of intuition in professional practice, and what he terms "slow ways of knowing" (Claxton, 1997) (see Chapter 7). Claxton regards intuition as a tool in reflective practice – involving expertise, judgement, sensitivity, creativity and rumination or pondering (Claxton, 2000). He suggests that we rely too much in modern society on rapid response – our hare brain – and too little on our tortoise mind, that allows for rumination, key to perception, understanding and reflection. This has particular relevance for the education of young children given the slower speed at which their brains operate and the under-development of the frontal lobes (see Chapter 8). Again it challenges mainstream thinking that pace is all – asking too many questions in too short a time cannot support the thinking and learning of very young children.

Continued ➤

9

Profile (cont.)

Claxton (2008a) highlights a range of approaches that stress *learning* rather than thinking:

- *Dispositions* rather than skills
- *Infusion* rather than stand-alone topics
- *Organic* rather than prescriptive methods
- *Involvement of students* rather than delivery of a ready-made product to them, and
- *Culture-shifting* rather than training.

Profile

Daniel Goleman

A number of less accessible, academic writers (see for example LeDoux, 1998) have written about the importance of emotions in learning but it is Goleman who has captured popular interest. The very terms *emotional intelligence* and *emotional literacy* invite confidence – helping what are often seen as soft or woolly aspects of human behaviour to be seen with increased regard. This is similar to the deference that MacNaughton describes in relation to neuroscience (see Chapter 8). Building on Howard Gardner's identification of two personal intelligences – namely the interpersonal (concerned with interacting with others) and intrapersonal (concerned with self-reflection) (Gardner, 1983), Goleman proposes an emotional intelligence (1996). He defines it as:

- Knowing one's feelings and using them to make good decisions in life
- Being able to manage moods and control impulses
- Being motivated and effectively overcoming setbacks in working towards goals.

(Pound, 2005: 79)

Gardner (1999) expresses some largely semantic concerns about whether emotionality can be an intelligence as he has defined them. One argument that Gardner puts forward is the fact that specifically identifying one intelligence as emotional suggests that there is no emotional aspect to other intelligences (although that could also be said of the two personal intelligences). Gardner (1999) also challenges Goleman on the grounds that he appears to recommend a set of behaviours which seem to be social policy or value judgements. These include empathy, considerateness, contribution to family or community life.

Figure 9.1 Children showing empathy

Carol Dweck

Carol Dweck is Professor of Psychology at Stanford University. She is perhaps best known to early childhood practitioners in this country for her work on "learned helplessness". This work was developed in the 1970s (Dweck, 1975). Put simply, those who believe that being clever is a fixed entity, regard failure as something they can do nothing about. Dweck (2000: 7) reports that those adopting what she calls the "helpless pattern" said things like "I'm no good at things like this" or "I guess I'm not very smart". However, those who believe that they can get better at something and can change lack of success are more likely to persist. Dweck (2000: 9) terms their approach "the mastery-oriented pattern" and highlights the absence of blame in their responses. She writes: "they didn't focus on reasons for the failures. In fact they didn't even seem to consider themselves to be failing". She reports them as saying things like "The harder it gets, the harder I need to try" and increasing their own motivation by articulating instructions to themselves.

Continued ➤

Profile (cont.)

Dweck's focus is on "why praising intelligence and ability doesn't foster self-esteem and lead to accomplishment, but may actually jeopardize success" (Pound, 2009: 25). Her self-theories (Dweck 2000) challenge a number of beliefs common to education and society:

- Students with high ability are often the students with the most concerns about failing.
- "Success in itself does little to boost students' desire for challenge or their ability to cope with setbacks" (Dweck, 2000: 1). It in fact is shown to do the reverse.
- "Praise can lead students to fear failure, avoid risks, doubt themselves … and cope poorly with setbacks" (Dweck, 2000: 2).
- "Many of the most confident individuals do not want their intelligence too stringently tested, and their high confidence is all too quickly shaken when they are confronted with difficulty" (Dweck, 2000: 2).

Key Debates

Can schools teach young children effectively?

Viewpoint: Government policy and the view of many members of our culture is that there are certain things that must be taught; knowledge to be acquired; curricula to be delivered.

Sources: Claxton, G. (2008b) *Cultivating Positive Learning Dispositions* (**www.guyclaxton.com/ documents/Routledge%20Companion%20to%20Ed%20chapter.pdf**)

House, R. (2011) *Too Much, Too Soon? Early Childhood and the Erosion of Childhood*. Stroud, Gloucs: Hawthorn Press.

Robinson, K. (2010) **www.ted.com/talks/ken_robinson_changing_education_paradigms.html**

Counter viewpoint: Claxton (2008b) highlights what is for him the futility of many current approaches to education. The idea that:

> "they must study Shakespeare and algebra" (or whatever is your favourite subject) because we are agreed that these are exemplary products of human learning and achievement, without paying any attention to the habits of mind that are being cultivated by 'studying' them in a particular way – and without asking whether those habits of mind are the ones they are going to need – is wildly irresponsible. The tedious to and fro between "traditionalists" and "progressives" that has passed for educational debate, and the woeful poverty

Continued ➤

of imagination that manifests as the current fascination with "personalisation" and "choice", are costly distractions because they usually leave the vital, prior questions of "why?", "what for?", unasked and unanswered.

The question raised by Willingham in Chapter 8 (2009) about the extent to which neuroscientists can be used to improve teaching and learning is one which should also be asked of politicians and policy-makers. The "habits of mind" to which Claxton refers are arguably of particular concern in the early years. Young children frequently demonstrate extremely positive learning dispositions such as curiosity (Claxton, 2008a), empathy (Trevarthen, 2011), an interest in representing ideas and feelings (Matthews, 2003) and so on. However, as Katz (1995, 2011) reminds us, if not nurtured in the early years, those dispositions will be extinguished and then prove difficult to reignite.

Similarly, Katz (2011) highlights the role that educators can and should play in strengthening and nurturing positive learning dispositions. Children should be helped to eradicate negative "habits of mind" which may have grown up. While this may seem obvious, all too often teachers and other educators complain about a child's lack of concentration, for example, but fail to plan to do anything to counter the negative disposition. Dowling (2010) reminds us, however, that a careful distinction must be made between negative learning dispositions and the characteristic learning at a particular age. She offers the example of the way in which a three-year-old "flitting" between activities and experiences should be judged quite differently from a five-year-old or a seven-year-old behaving in the same way.

Research into willpower or cognitive control (see Mischel at al., 2011) is of interest in thinking about ways to support positive dispositions. The original experiments done in the 1960s, involved confronting young children with a marshmallow and promising them another if they could resist eating for a short period while the researcher was out of the room. If you are not familiar with these experiments you can get a flavour of them (the experiments rather than the marshmallows that is) by viewing a short film on **www.eatmedaily. com/2009/09/psychological-experiments-in-self-control-the-marshmallow-test/**. Mischel et al. (2011) suggest that over a period of 40 years, children's response to this test had a high rate of prediction in indicating children who may have cognitive and mental health problems. The more immediate outcomes, which they also seemed to predict, were significantly different SAT scores in elementary school.

The author of New Zealand's *Learning Stories* (Carr, 2001) has continued to focus on the vital importance of learning dispositions in practice (see for example Carr and Lee, 2012 and Carr et al., 2009). If they can do it despite the concerns of politicians and policy-makers (Smith, 2011) so can others. Education for young children must take a long-term view, supporting not just learning content in the short term but nurturing children's disposition to learn throughout their lives. Moreover, practitioners should reflect on whether "the dispositions we want to encourage and support in the children we teach can be seen by them in us?" (Katz, 2011: 122).

Research Methods

The diversity of the theorists and practitioners involved in thinking about learning dispositions makes it impossible that there would be anything other than a very wide range of research methods associated with them. Dweck for example uses interview techniques with large samples of schoolchildren. Goleman (1996) draws on a range of empirical studies while Rogers drew largely on his psychotherapeutic insights.

Claxton, in common with many other theorists, employs a battery of research methods; draws on a range of research findings but places them all in framework of beliefs and values that allow him to weigh up and pay attention to the research or discount it. In an article entitled *Cultivating Positive Learning Dispositions* (2008b), he outlines the importance of three particular research approaches which he terms "sands", to which must be added "visionary cement" (a vision of what schools and education might be like to live up to in the 21st century) and the "water" of action research – in order to build firm foundations for learning. Only the small-scale, practical and contextually focused research projects associated with action research can, he believes, achieve the changes needed to support the development of learning dispositions.

The "building sands" he proposes are cognitive science; neuroscience and socio-cultural psychology. Of the first he writes:

> From cognitive science comes, crucially, a reappraisal of our understanding of the nature of "intelligence". Out has gone the idea that young people's learning is largely determined by a fixed-sized pot of general purpose resource which they inherited from their parents – a factor over which teachers therefore have no control. And in has come a growing realisation of the extent to which *learning reflects habits of mind that have themselves been learned*, and which are therefore amenable in principle to further growth or change. On this new view, it becomes possible for teachers to see themselves as "mind coaches": people who are in the business not only of transmitting "bodies of knowledge, skill and understanding", but of expanding the capacity to learn itself.

He highlights the strengths of neuroscience but warns that "we have to be careful, however, as it has become contaminated. There is a good deal of uncritical hype about 'brain-based learning' at the moment". He also warns that "thinking too much" gets in the way of learning, arguing that knowing this, teachers can help their students to develop an appreciation of when and how to pay wordless attention, as well as when and how to analyse and explain.

Claxton also draws attention to a new of field of study – "affective neuroscience". He adds that neuroscientists are finding that emotions are an essential element of intelligence or cognition, adding

Continued ➤

Research Methods (cont.)

that, "emotional intelligence seems to be much more a matter of understanding the vital functions of emotions, and heeding their messages, than of trying to 'manage them away'".

Claxton goes on to outline the contribution of the socio-cultural constructivist theories of Vygotsky, who he sees as offering two distinct insights. The first emphasises the impact of modelling learning characteristics. Second, learning is shaped by the learner's "habits of mind" and on the cultural tools to hand but above all on "the intricate, evanescent web of human resources in which I am always enmeshed".

In Practice

On the whole, the theories which emphasise the role of learning dispositions in developing and supporting cognition are rooted in practice. The theorists involved generally appear to have a particular interest in education and like Goleman and Claxton may actually be focusing on why things aren't working better within schools and other educational establishments. Thus, their theories are having a strong impact on educationalists – though perhaps insufficient influence on policy-makers and politicians.

A number of issues for practice are raised when focusing on dispositions for learning:
- The idea of child-centred or learner-centred education has long been a tenet of early childhood education. The term child-centred education is often associated with Piaget and has received much criticism. However, Rogers' use of the term learner-centred has lent respectability. It is connected to an early childhood approach, favoured by EYFS (DfE, 2012), of a child-led curriculum and to education more broadly through individualised or personalised programmes. The notion of teacher as facilitator also comes from Rogers (1983).
- Reflective practice was advocated by John Dewey who believed there to be five distinct stages in critical reflection (see Pollard, 2002). In the 21st century reflective practice is seen as a vital element of professionalism (see Gardner, 2006a). For Claxton (2008a), reflection is also an important part of effective educational practice.
- Ferre Laevers' work on involvement and well-being has been widely adopted. His rating scales have given an air of respectability to what can otherwise be seen as "soft" measures. They are part of the EEL project and have been firmly adopted in influential children's centres such as Pen Green. These ideas are further supported by Daniel Goleman's (1996) work where he advocates environments for well-being which emphasise emotional safety and security, stimulation, tasks and activities which have real-life meaning and feedback which promotes well-being. Goleman's ideas are often framed as supporting emotional literacy and taken up in schools on that basis. The work of Gerhardt (2004) and Palmer (2006) also underlines the importance of nurturing well-being.

Continued ➤

In Practice (cont.)

- What Dweck's work (2000) shows clearly is the importance of specific praise rather than general comments about how nice something that a child has done is or how clever he or she is to have done it. Specific praise has the advantage (in addition to the advantages set out by Dweck, 2000) of enabling children to see how to repeat their success. "I like the colours you have chosen for your painting – they go really well together" is more effective than "Wow what a great painting!" Dweck's work also underlines the belief that all learning involves error, that we should not be afraid of it and should enable children to welcome challenge – secure in the notion that they can develop cognitive skills to help them address challenges.

Next Steps

Carr, M., Smith, A. and Duncan, J. (2010) *Learning in the Making: Disposition and Design in Early Education.* Rotterdam: Sense Publications.

House, R. (2011) *Too Much, Too Soon? Early Childhood and the Erosion of Childhood.* Stroud, Gloucs: Hawthorn Press.

Glossary

Affective neuroscience: the study of the neural mechanisms of emotion. This interdisciplinary field combines neuroscience with the psychological study of personality, emotion and mood.

Summary

In undertaking an assignment on cognition you may like to consider making reference to some of the key issues explored in this chapter, including:

- there is as yet no overall consensus on what are the most important learning dispositions. However, there is widespread agreement among psychologists and practitioners on the importance of personal, social and emotional aspects of learning.
- this approach has been addressed in some parts of the world but it is disappointing that despite the government's rhetoric about prime areas of learning and development there is continued emphasis on tests, such as the phonics screening, which undermine it.

Complex Human Learning – Narrative, Imagination, Music and Creative Thinking

Introduction

As we saw in Chapter 1, cognition is made up of many facets of human thought – reasoning, intuition, perception, attention, language, problem-solving, creativity, deduction and decision-making. Language has not been explored in this book since it is such a vast subject that it will require a book of its own. Similarly, the subject of play undoubtedly deserves a place here but will also be the topic of a book in its own right within this series. However, in this chapter the focus will be on other aspects of cognition which seem to be of particular current interest and which may be thought of as elements of creative thinking.

This chapter covers aspects of the work of:
● Ken Robinson
● Vivian Gussin Paley.

It also highlights key debates around:
● Young children and creativlty
● Knowing minds.

In the beginning

This chapter, devoted to complex human learning, begins with a puzzle – the connection that babies make with adults and the role of adults in drawing the baby into the culture.

10

Key Debates

?!

Knowing minds

Viewpoint: Deconstructionists like Burman (1994: 36) challenge the notion of an "innate predisposition to be social". She argues that the social motives attributed to young babies do not exist but are created in the mind of the researcher. She rejects the view that the baby contributes to the shared interaction established through attachment. Human psychology, those holding this view suggest, is essentially about individual components or aspects of cognition such as intelligence, perception and so on. For them, social interactions and emotions may modify or alter these components but remain of less importance than the components themselves.

Sources: Burman, E. (1994) *Deconstructing Developmental Psychology*. London: Routledge (see Chapter 3).

Reddy, V. (2008) *How Infants Know Minds*. London: Harvard University Press.

Counter viewpoint: Trevarthen and many other psychologists (as well as parents and practitioners) refute any idea that babies are not innately social. Reddy (2008: 233), for example, writes:

> Infants seem to be capable of entering into dialogue with other people remarkably early in life. From birth they prefer to look at faces which engage them in direct mutual gaze, and they are capable of engaging in imitative exchanges that reveal not just an ability to recognise similarity between self and other but a motivation to invite engagement. Within two months of birth, infants become more robust at dialogic exchanges with people, showing not only prolonged turn-taking and sensitive detection of the contingency and relevance of others' responses, but a sensitivity to many emotional nuances.

Trevarthen (2008: 24) also rejects the view that human thinking and behaviour can usefully be broken down into individual components. He writes:

> innate, intuitive powers of the mind in a brain that moves the thousands of muscles in the body with such sensitive awareness of what will happen, are not properly understood by a psychology that accepts a model of consciousness, intelligence and personality, that focuses only on the cognitive processing of information. A richer, more common sense philosophy is gaining ground ... Every live human person has some of this intuitive capacity to share intentions and feelings, and to make friends.

Continued ➤

The notion that social interactions make cognition possible is borne out in the work of many theorists. This insight is not exclusive to developmental psychology. It is, for example, apparent in the work of:

- Rogers (1983), a humanistic psychologist, who writes of the importance of "unconditional positive regard" between teacher and taught, therapist and client.
- Siegel (1999), a clinical psychiatrist, who writes of the importance of attachment in establishing what he calls "mindsight" – getting in touch with other minds in developing cognition.
- Ramachandran (2011), a neuroscientist, who explores the importance of mirror neurons in human interaction and learning.

In short there is much reason to believe that the infants' propensity for social behaviour is linked to cognition. In fact there is also evidence to link the social basis of cognition with imagination, music and complex learning such as creativity.

Creativity and creative thinking

Ramachandran and Blakeslee (1999: 197) describe creativity as "an ineffable quality ... which brings us face to face with the very essence of what it is to be human". Evolutionary psychologists believe creativity to have emerged in humans around 45,000 years ago (Lewis-Williams, 2002), a period known as the *human revolution* or the *creative explosion*. Lewis-Williams suggests that the changes in human thinking and behaviour which supported this explosion included the emergence of abstract thought and the development of symbolic behaviour, group behaviour and the development of tools.

Profile

Ken Robinson

Ken Robinson is based at the University of Warwick. He chaired the government committee that published a report, *All our Futures,* on creativity in education (NACCCE, 1999). Little was heard of it until the publication of *Excellence and Enjoyment* (DfES, 2003). In *All our Futures* creativity is defined as "imaginative activity fashioned so as to produce outcomes that are both original and of value" (NACCCE, 1999: 30). Thus the following characteristics are defined as being of importance:

—— Continued ➤

Profile (cont.)

- *Imagination* – may be defined as "possibility thinking" (Craft, 2002), "what if thinking" or "a miracle of human experience" (Jenkinson, 2001: 58, citing Singer and Singer, 1990).
- *Purposeful activity* – purposeful activity does not necessarily mean a pre-determined purpose. Much creative behaviour arises from the inspiration of a randomly drawn line or the shape of some recycled material; for example, the muzzle of the famous prehistoric cave painting of a horse in Pech Merle in France, which uses a piece of rock with a muzzle-shape as the starting point. (See **www. bing.com/images/search?q=pech+merle+cave+art+pics&qpvt=pech+merle+cave+art+ pics&FORM=IQFRML**. The horse in question is the spotted horse on the far right.) Children, expert artists and designers often use this approach.
- *Originality* – this may seem difficult to find in young children. Robinson suggests three levels of originality – personal, social and historic. Bruce (2004) offers a similar interpretation describing the three types as everyday, specialist and world-shattering creators. Rogoff (1990) highlights the social aspect of creativity – describing creative ideas as making connections between old and unfamiliar thoughts. In addition she argues that, "individual creativity occurs in the context of a community of thinkers … Where more than one person is working on the solution of a particular problem" (Rogoff, 1990: 198).
- *Critical awareness* – this involves thinking about thinking – a human trait which enables us to learn from our mistakes and build on our successes.

Ken Robinson continues to speak on and to publish in the field of creativity and, like Guy Claxton, is seeking ways to change schools (**www.ted.com/talks/ken_robinson_says_schools_kill_creativity.html**). *Out of our Minds: Learning to be Creative* (Robinson, 2011) is highly readable. On his website there are a number of videos of him talking on the subject of creativity and its importance to the future of the human race. In the preface to the revised edition he states that, "We will not succeed in navigating the complex environment of the future by peering relentlessly into a rear view mirror. To do so we would be out of our minds" (Robinson, 2011: xii). You can also see Robinson talking about the need for creativity on **www.ted.com/speakers/ sir_ken_robinson.html**. His theme is that we are "educating people out of their creativity".

Key Debates

Young children and creativity

Viewpoint: It is suggested that what we see in children is merely novelty – not creativity (Sawyer et al., 2003). Czikszentmihalyi (2003: 217) suggests that "creativity can only be defined in a system that includes domain and field" and cannot therefore be found in young children. He defines a *domain* as "a set of symbolic

———————————————————————————————— Continued ➤

rules and procedures" such as mathematics (1997: 27) and a *field* as "the individuals who act as gatekeepers to the field" (1997: 28). Czikszentmihalyi illustrates his viewpoint by outlining who the gatekeepers might be in the field of visual art – critics, curators and so on. He goes on to give some more unusual examples (1997: 43):

> For some domains, the field is as broad as society itself. It took the entire population of the United States to decide whether the recipe for New Coke was an innovation worth keeping. On the other hand, it has been said that only four or five people in the world initially understood Einstein's theory of relativity, but their opinion had enough weight to make his name a household word.

Sources: Czikszentmihalyi, M. (1997) *Creativity: Flow and the Psychology of Discovery and Invention*. New York: HarperPerennial.

Fumoto et al. (2012) *Young Children's Creative Thinking*. London: Sage.

Sawyer et al. (2003) *Creativity and Development*. Oxford: Oxford University Press.

Counter viewpoint: One is tempted to argue that despite being a seminal writer on the subject of creativity, Czikszentmihalyi has insufficient knowledge of young children's cognition. This is a pity because he highlights factors which might be applied to young children. He refers to *autotelic* activity – things we do simply for the joy of the experience and which contribute to creativity. He contrasts this with *exotelic* activity – things we do for some future goal or with a particular motive.

Key to this debate is that creativity like other forms of cognition is a developmental process. Fumoto et al. (2012) suggest that creative thinking is an indicator of developing creativity and can therefore be used to promote its likelihood in children. They also suggest that educators, by observing and developing the characteristics of creative thinking, will be able to nurture it. Hargreaves (2012) cites three motivations identified by Sternberg as indicators of creative thinking – namely the motivation to take on new challenges; to engage in things that are enjoyed and enjoyable; and to be sufficiently motivated to persist. He goes on to propose (Hargreaves, 2012: 18) that:

> certain types of behaviour indicate creative thinking in young children and that creative thinking is a predictor of real life creativity when linked with optimal environmental conditions, and appropriate levels of motivation and persistence.

Research into children's creative thinking

The behaviours that predict creativity and indicate creative thinking (Fumoto et al., 2012) are set out in the Analysing Children's Creative Thinking (ACCT) (Robson, 2012). Three categories of behaviour are identified and each has a number of indicators. The behaviours are as follows:

Continued ➤

Key Debates (cont.) _____ ?!

- *Exploration*, consisting of exploring; engaging in new activity; and knowing what you want to do.
- *Involvement and enjoyment,* which includes trying out; analysing ideas; speculating; and involving others.
- *Persistence,* in which children are seen to be persisting; risk-taking and completing challenges – the latter importantly refers to "conscious awareness of his/her own thinking" (Robson, 2012: 95) or metacognition.

The ACCT is particularly important as a tool for thinking about young children's thinking. The issue of originality is one obstacle. Similarly, Gardner (2006b: 177) talks about "the quality of their products" – again difficult to achieve at the age or three (or even six). What is clear about high-quality products – however they are defined and in whatever mode or medium we are considering – is that they come about through hours and hours of practice. Ten thousand hours of practice is what is needed to become an expert (Howe, 1999) and as Sloboda intimates (1985) children will only engage to such a high level when experiences and activities offer fun and/ or emotional satisfaction.

Craft (2002) highlights the concept of "possibility thinking" and its role in what she terms "little 'c' creativity" – akin to Bruce's (2004) everyday creativity. Gardner (2006a: 84) comments on the creativity demonstrated by young children prior to entering formal schooling. He argues that children of this age make more and more unusual connections than at any other time of life (1993b). He suggests that Picasso declared that "I used to draw like Raphael; it has taken me my whole life to learn to draw like a child" (2006b: 84). His description (2006b: 84) of the "creative powers" of a five-year-old will strike a chord with many involved in the care and education of young children:

> Given even a modestly supportive environment, youngsters are not only intrigued by a wide range of phenomena, experiences, topics, and questions; they persist in exploring, even in the absence of encouragement, let alone material rewards. Few are the children who are not galvanized by a trip to a county fair, an amusement park, or a children's museum; their playfulness, curiosity, and imaginative powers are palpable.

Music and the impact of musicality

Mithen (2005: vii) has suggested that "the propensity to make music is the most mysterious, wonderful and neglected feature of humankind". He describes the way in which music has, in the past, often been overlooked or marginalised by academics and researchers. As a professor of prehistory he berates himself for his earlier failure to understand its importance. He dismisses Steven Pinker's much publicised view (1994) that music is "something that humans have invented merely as entertainment" (Mithen, 2005: 5). He highlights the views of a range of musicologists and music educators that:

- Music is critical to children's cognitive development.
- Music is a symbolic activity and involves physical action. Music, like play, allows children to explore what they can do – but although play-based action such as rough and tumble play and dance may have similarities, movement in response to music is said to involve higher-order thinking (Panksepp and Trevarthen, 2009).
- The "instinct to sing" is as powerful as the "instinct to speak". Musical elements, which include the pitch and loudness of the voice, are among the earliest representations or as Papousek (1994) suggests the baby's voice is his or her first toy.
- The evolution of language included a musical phase.
- Human evolution included a period involving "nonverbal, prelinguistic, 'musical' mode(s) of thought and action" (Mithen, 2005: 5).

Story, play and imagination

In writings about creativity and about music, play and imagination are seen as having an important role. The work of Vivian Gussin Paley is of particular interest to early childhood practitioners, highlighting as she does the narratives and meanings that emerge from children's play and stories. However, she is by no means alone in this enthusiasm. Haven (2007: 13) defines stories as "our universal storehouse of knowledge, beliefs, values, attitudes, passions, dreams, imagination and vision". He adds that "stories … drive the mental processes that lead to understanding, to the creation of meaning, context and relevance; and to active memory" (2007: 80). In short, stories, like play and imagination, contribute to thinking and cognition.

Figure 10.1 Imaginative thinking: story acting

Profile

Vivian Gussin Paley

Vivian Gussin Paley was part of an immigrant family from eastern Europe and grew up in Chicago. Throughout her working life she taught early childhood settings including the University of Chicago Laboratory Schools. Her many books are essentially her observations, recordings and transcriptions of children's interactions and conversations in those settings, together with her analysis of what she has seen and heard.

Probably the best-known aspect of her work is her story-telling/story-acting approach and because of this she is often associated with the development of language in young children. It is true to say that a love of story and theatre undoubtedly offer a strong motivation (Lee, 2011). Building on her belief in narrative, Paley (2004: 8) asserts that play is "mankind's oldest and best-used learning tool"; and that "fantasy play and story-making [are] the original learning tools that children use to understand and make sense of the world" (Lee 2011: 122, citing Paley).

We learn in *The Boy Who Would be a Helicopter* (Paley, 1990) that transcribing her recordings of children and events in her classroom was her daily task. If you have ever undertaken any transcription you will know what a massive undertaking that was. Her books do not make academic references but are challenging and inspiring. Her pedagogy includes story-writing/story-acting – an activity in which she scribes children's stories and then at the end of each day they are acted out by the children. She links this to her purpose (Paley, 2004: 3) explaining:

> In documenting and dramatizing their language, lore, and literary strivings, my purpose is to examine their curriculum in its natural form, much as they study one another through the medium of their play.

Cooper (2009) suggests that Paley's true legacy is to encourage teachers of young children to challenge received wisdom about what young children should be doing. Lee (2011: 122–3) identifies Paley's key qualities from which she believes practitioners should learn. These include:

- *A curiosity for asking questions and finding answers* ... concerning the children in her class and their relationships with each other and the outside world ... One of the major questions she constantly refers to concerns fairness...
- *A belief in the wisdom of children* ... [reflected in] her desire to understand the words, thoughts and actions of everyone in her class...
- *A non-judgemental approach.*

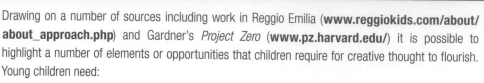

Drawing on a number of sources including work in Reggio Emilia (**www.reggiokids.com/about/about_approach.php**) and Gardner's *Project Zero* (**www.pz.harvard.edu/**) it is possible to highlight a number of elements or opportunities that children require for creative thought to flourish. Young children need:

- rich opportunities for imaginative play
- social interaction since it requires negotiation
- exploration
- the use of a diverse range of media which can be used to represent or symbolise experience, ideas and feelings
- sustained conversations which support them in making connections with past experiences and value the unusual connections which they make (Gardner, 2006)
- support to enjoy experiencing the unexpected.

They also need adults who:

- ensure plenty of time and space, and its flexible use
- provide a secure environment that encourages children to take and manage risk safely
- encourage children to make choices and experience the impact of their decisions
- promote in children, diligence and exuberance or persistence and playfulness.

The revised EYFS (DfE, 2012) replaces the area of learning and development formerly known as creative development, with one called expressive arts and design. This is to be welcomed as it will help to remove any doubt that creativity might be confined to the arts. As Lucas (2001: 38) reminds us:

> Creativity is a state of mind in which all of our intelligences are working together. It involves seeing, thinking and innovating. Although it is found in the creative arts, creativity can be found in any subject at school or in any aspect of life.

There is some congruence between the characteristics of effective learning (DfE, 2012; Stewart, 2012) and characteristics of creative thinking (Fumoto and Robson, 2012: 7). Key words drawn from both documents include:

- *Exploring*: finding out, engaging in new activity, trying things out, risk-taking
- *Persistence*: keeping on trying, concentrating, being involved
- *Thinking*: choosing, knowing what you want to do, analysing ideas, speculating, conscious awareness of your own thinking, involving others
- *Enjoyment*.

Continued ➤

In Practice (cont.)

Music, dance, play and imagination

All too often these are marginalised areas of the curriculum. There is strong evidence that at every level of education, their importance should be recognised. Parents need to be aware of their role in engaging with young children musically and playfully. Early years practitioners can have confidence in the importance of nurturing aspects such as enjoyment, playfulness and excitement. Cooper (2009: 156), writing about the work of Vivian Gussin Paley, cites teachers who "talked … about learning to be a teacher of children first, and a teacher of academics second [and] to resist what didn't make sense in the lives of the children". These are important lessons for practice.

Research Methods

Researchers such as Trevarthen and Reddy rely for their research on video recording to a large extent. Paley, as we have seen, makes use of audio recording. In both cases careful observation is followed by detailed analysis. For Paley, the analysis is woven into the narrative of the texts she writes. For Trevarthen and Reddy, the analyses are subjected to different forms of statistical analysis, which allow them to weave their own stories – linking new information to previous findings.

Analysing children's creative thinking

In order to carry out their research, Fumoto et al. (2012) developed a framework (ACCT) through which to analyse their narrative observations. They did this because they rejected the more usual test of young children's creativity – the Torrance Test of Creative Thinking. Their reasons included:

- its focus on originality which they regard as just one measure of creative thinking, not a reliable indicator of creativity or creative thinking as a whole
- its reliance on communicative responses which may not be a fair representation of children's cognitive ability
- the fact that it relies on a test or disembedded situation which does not allow children to demonstrate their full ability or competence (Donaldson, 1978).

Fumoto et al. (2012) also felt that any analysis of children's creative thinking should involve reflective dialogue with practitioners and children. Video footage obtained for the study was shown to children and their key person. Sustained, shared conversations often ensued. Robson (2012: 59) reports that:

> The discussions afforded children the opportunity to display their knowledge, often in ways which might otherwise have remained invisible to the adults. Importantly, this supports the pedagogical value of video reflection, for teaching and learning as well as research.

Next Steps

Reddy, V. (2008) *How Infants Know Minds.* London: Harvard University Press.

Robinson, K. (2011) *Out of our Minds: Learning to be Creative.* Chichester: Capstone Publishing Ltd.

Glossary

Autotelic activity: things we do simply for the joy of the experience and which contribute to creativity.

Exotelic activity: things we do for some future goal or with a particular motive.

Summary

In undertaking an assignment on the complexity of human learning and its early beginnings you may like to consider making reference to some of the underlying issues explored in this chapter, including:

- the social and creative abilities of young children
- the importance of playful, joyful behaviour and excitement in learning
- the role of music in promoting social interaction.

References

Addy, L. (2004) *Speed Up! A Kinaesthetic Programme to Develop Fluent Handwriting.* Oxford: Blackwell.

Athey, C. (1990) *Extending Thought in Young Children.* London: Paul Chapman.

Auden, W.H. (1977) *The Portable Greek Reader.* Harmondsworth: Penguin Books.

Baars, B. (1986) *The Cognitive Revolution in Psychology.* New York: Guilford Press.

Barker, R. (2011) *Every Child Matters and the Coalition Government.* e-book.

Bartsch, K. and Wellman, H. (1995) *Children Talk About the Mind.* Oxford: Oxford University Press.

Blakemore, C. (1982) 'Developmental plasticity in the brain: a parable for education', in The Brain Sciences and Education. Symposium conducted in January at the American Association for the Advancement of Science. Washington DC.

Blakemore, S-J. and Frith, U. (2005) *The Learning Brain.* Oxford: Blackwell Publishing.

Bower, T. (1977a) 'Babies are More Important than Machines', New Scientist, 74 (1057): 712.

Bower, T. (1977b) *The Perceptual World of the Child.* Glasgow: Fontana.

Bower, T. (1982) *Development in Infancy* (2nd ed.). San Francisco: W.H. Freeman.

BBC (2009) 'Social websites: bad for kids' brains?'. BBC Newsnight, 25 February 2009. **http://news.bbc.co.uk/1/hi/programmes/newsnight/7909847.stm.** Retrieved 15 June 2012.

Bronfenbrenner, U. (1979) *The Ecology of Human Development.* London: Harvard University Press.

Bronfenbrenner, U. (2004) (First published 1971) *Making Human Beings.* London: Sage.

Brooks, R. (1991) 'Intelligence Without Representation', Artificial Intelligence, 47: 139–59.

Brown, R. (1973) *A First Language: The Early Stages.* London: Allen and Unwin.

Bruce, T. (2004) *Cultivating Creativity in Babies, Toddlers and Young Children.* London: Hodder.

Bruce, T. (2011) *Early Childhood Education* (4th ed.). London: Hodder.

Bruer, J. (1999) *The Myth of the First Three Years.* New York: The Free Press.

Bruner, J. (1960) *The Process of Education.* Boston MA. Harvard University Press.

Bruner, J. (1965) *Man: A Course of Study.* Watertown, MA: Educational Services Inc.

Bruner, J. (1980) *Under Five in Britain.* London: Grant McIntyre Ltd.

Bruner, J. (1981) 'What is representation?', in M. Roberts, and J. Tamburrini (eds) *Child Development 0–5.* Edinburgh: Holmes McDougall.

Bruner, J. (1983) *Child's Talk.* Oxford: Oxford University Press.

Bruner, J. (1986) *Actual Minds, Possible Worlds.* London: Harvard University Press.

Bruner, J. (1996) *The Culture of Education.* Cambridge MA: Harvard University Press.

Bruner, J. (2003) *Making Stories: Law, Literature and Life.* Cambridge MA: Harvard University Press.

Burman, E. (1994) *Deconstructing Developmental Psychology.* London: Routledge.

Calvin, W. (1997) *How Brains Think.* London: Weidenfeld and Nicolson.

Carr, M. (2001) *Assessment in Early Childhood Settings: Learning Stories.* London: Paul Chapman Publishing.

Carr, M. and Lee, W. (2012) *Learning Stories: Constructing Learner Identities in Early Education.* London: Sage.

Carr, M., Smith, A. and Duncan, J. (2010) *Learning in the Making: Disposition and Design in Early Education.* Rotterdam: Sense Publications.

Carroll, J. (1993) *Human Cognitive Abilities*. Cambridge: Cambridge University Press.

Ceci, S. (1996) *On Intelligence*. London: Harvard University Press.

Chen, J., Krechevsky, M. and Viens, J. (1998) *Building on Children's Strengths: The Experience of Project Spectrum*. Teachers' College Press.

Chomsky, N. (1959) 'Review of Verbal Behavior by B.F. Skinner', *Language*, 35 (1) 26–58.

Chomsky, N. (2006) *Language and Mind* (3rd ed.). Cambridge: Cambridge University Press.

Claxton, G. (1985) 'Educational Psychology: what is it trying to prove?', in G. Claxton, W. Swann, P. Salmon, V. Walkerdine, B. Jacobsen and J. White, *Psychology and Schooling: What's the Matter?* London: Bedford Way Papers.

Claxton, G. (1997) *Hare Brain: Tortoise Mind*. London: Fourth Estate.

Claxton, G. (2000) 'The anatomy of intuition', in T. Atkinson and G. Claxton (eds) *The Intuitive Practitioner*. Buckingham: Open University Press.

Claxton, G. (2008a) *What's the Point of School?* Oxford: Oneworld Publications.

Claxton, G. (2008b) *Cultivating positive learning dispositions* **www.guyclaxton.com/documents/Routledge%20Companion%20to%20Ed%20chapter.pdf** Accessed 3 June 2012.

Cohen, D. (2002) *How the Child's Mind Develops*. London: Routledge.

Cole, M. and Scribner, M. (1974) *Culture and Thought: A Psychological Introduction*. New York: Wiley.

Costall, A. (2004) 'From direct perception to the primacy of action: a closer look at James Gibson's ecological approach to psychology', in G. Bremner and A. Slater (eds) *Theories of Infant Development*. Oxford: Blackwell Publishing Ltd.

Cooper, P. (2009) *The Classrooms all Young Children Need – Lessons in Teaching from Vivian Paley*. London: The University of Chicago Press Ltd.

Craft, A. (2002) *Creativity and Early Years Education: A Lifewide Foundation*. London: Continuum Press.

Czikszentmihalyi, M. (1997) *Creativity: Flow and the Psychology of Discovery and Invention*. New York: HarperPerennial.

Daniels, H., Cole, M. and Wertsch, J. (eds) (2007) *The Cambridge Companion to Vygotsky*. Cambridge; Cambridge University Press.

Darling, N. (2007) 'Ecological Systems Theory: The Person in the Center of the Circles', *Research in Human Development* 4(3–4): 203–17.

Department for Education (DfE) (2012) *Statutory Framework for the Early Years Foundation Stage: Setting the standards for learning, development and care for children from birth to five* **www.foundationyears.org.uk** or **www.education.gov.uk**.

Department for Education and Science (DfES) (2003) *Excellence and Enjoyment. London*: DfES.

Derbyshire, David (24 February 2009). London: Daily Mail. **www.dailymail.co.uk/news/article-1153583/Social-websites-harm-childrens-brains-Chilling-warning-parents-neuroscientist.html** Accessed 3 June 2012.

Devlin, K. (2000) *The Maths Gene*. London: Weidenfeld and Nicolson.

Dewey, J. (1910) *How We Think*. Cincinatti, OH: LLC Publishers.

Donaldson, M. (1978) *Children's Minds*. London: Fontana.

Dowling, M. (2010) *Young Children's Personal, Social and Emotional Development* (3rd ed.). London: Sage.

Drummond, M-J., and Jenkinson, S. (2009) *Meeting the Child: Approaches to Observation and Assessment in Steiner Kindergartens*. Plymouth: University of Plymouth/ Steiner Waldorf Early Years Research Group.

Dweck, C. (1975) 'The Role of Expectations and Attributions in the Alleviation of Learned Helplessness', Journal of Personality and Social Psychology, 31, 674–85.

Dweck, C. (2000) *Self-theories: Their Role in Motivation, Personality and Development*. Hove: Psychology Press.

Eccles, J. and Appleton, J. (2002) *Community Programs to Promote Youth Development*. Washington DC: National Academies Press.

Egan, K. (1991) *Primary Understanding*. London: Routledge.

Eliot, L. (1999) *Early Intelligence*. London: Penguin Books Ltd.

Eysenck, M. and Keane, M. (2010) *Cognitive Psychology: A Student's Handbook* (6th ed.). Hove, E. Sussex: Psychology Press.

Faules, D. and Alexander D (1978) *Communication and social behaviour: a symbolic interaction perspective*. Reading, Mass.: Addison Wesley.

Flavell, J., Green, F. and Flavell, E. (1990) 'Developmental Changes in Young Children's Knowledge About the Mind', *Cognitive Development*, January 1990 5,1: 1–27.

Fleck, J. (1982). 'Development and establishment in artificial intelligence', in N. Elias, H. Martins and R. Whitley (eds) *Scientific Establishments and Hierarchies*. Holland: D. Reidel.

Flynn, J. (2009) *What is Intelligence?* Cambridge: Cambridge University Press ebook.

Fodor, J. (1983) *The Modularity of Mind*. Cambridge MA: MIT Press.

Fumoto, H. and Robson, S. (2012) 'Social relationships in early childhood', in H. Fumoto, S. Robson, S. Greenfield and D. Hargreaves (eds) *Young Children's Creative Thinking*. London: Sage.

Fumoto, H., Robson, S., Greenfield, S. and Hargreaves, D. (2012) *Young Children's Creative Thinking*. London: Sage.

Freund, L. (1990) 'Maternal Regulation of Children's Problem-solving Behaviour and its Impact on Children's Performance', *Child Development* 61(1): 113–26.

Fry, P. (1984) 'Teachers' conceptions of students' intelligence and intelligent functioning: a cross-sectional study of elementary, secondary and tertiary level teachers', in P. Fry (ed.) *Changing Conceptions of Intelligence and Intellectual Functioning*. New York: North-Holland.

Gardner, H. (1983) *Frames of Mind: The Theory of Multiple Intelligence*. New York: Basic Books.

Gardner, H (1989) *To Open Minds*. New York: Basic Books.

Gardner, H. (1993a) *Frames of Mind* (2nd ed.). London: Pan Books.

Gardner, H (1993b) *The Unschooled Mind*. London: Fontana.

Gardner, H. (1999) *Intelligence Reframed*. New York: Perseus Books.

Gardner, H. (2001) Jerome S Bruner, in J. Palmer (ed.) *Fifty Modern Thinkers on Education*. London: Routledge.

Gardner, H. (2006a) *Five Minds for the Future*. Boston, MA: Harvard Business School Press.

Gardner, H. (2006b) *Multiple Intelligences: New Horizons*. New York: Basic Books.

Gardner, H., Feldman, D. and Krechevsky, M. (eds). (1998) *Project Zero Frameworks for Early Childhood Education*. New York: Teachers College Press.

Gardner, H., Kornhaber, M. and Wake, W. (1996) *Intelligence: Multiple Perspectives*. Orlando, FL: Harcourt Brace and Company.

Gerhardt, S. (2004) *Why Love Matters*. Hove, E. Sussex: Brunner-Routledge.

Goldacre (2010) **http://bengoldacre.posterous.com**

Goldacre, Ben (21 October 2011) 'Serious claims belong in a serious scientific paper', the Guardian (London). **www.guardian.co.uk/commentisfree/2011/oct/21/bad-science-publishing-claims**. Accessed 10 June 2012.

Goleman, D. (1996) *Emotional Intelligence.* London: Bloomsbury Publishing.

Gopnik, A., Melttzoff, A. and Kuhl, P. (1990) *How Babies Think.* London: Weidenfeld and Nicolson.

Goswami, U. (2004) 'Neuroscience and education', British Journal of Educational Psychology. 1–14 March, 74 (1).

Gould, S. J. (2007) *The Richness of Life.* London: Vintage Press.

Gray, C. and MacBlain, S. (2012) *Learning Theories in Childhood.* London: Sage.

Greenfield, S. (1996) *The Human Mind Explained.* London: Cassell Publishers Ltd.

Greenfield, S. (1997) *The Human Brain: A Guided Tour.* London: Weidenfeld and Nicolson.

Greenfield, S. (2007) 'Style without substance', Times Educational Supplement. 27/7/07, page 25.

Greenfield, S. (2009) *ID: The quest for meaning in the 21st century.* London: Hodder.

Greenland, P. (2000) *Hopping Home Backwards: Body Intelligence and Movement Play.* London: Jabadao.

Guidici, C., Rinaldi, C. and Krechevsky, M. (2001) *Making Learning Visible.* Reggio: Project Zero and Reggio Children.

Haddon, M. (2004) *The Curious Incident of the Dog in the Night-time.* London: Vintage.

Haggbloom S.J. (2002) 'The 100 Most Eminent Psychologists of the 20th Century', Review of General Psychology, 6 (2): 139–52.

Hargreaves, D. (2012) 'What do we mean by creativity and creative thinking?', in H. Fumoto, S. Robson, S. Greenfield, and D. Hargeaves, *Young Children's Creative Thinking.* London: Sage.

Haven, K. (2007) *Story Proof.* Westport CT: Libraries Unlimited.

Holland, P. (2003) *We Don't Play With Guns Here.* Maidenhead: Open University Press.

House, R. (2011) (ed.) *Too Much, Too Soon?* Early Learning and the Erosion of Childhood. Stroud, Gloucs: Hawthorn Press.

Howe, M. (1999) *Genius Explained.* Cambridge: Cambridge University Press.

Hughes, M. and Grieve, R. (1983) 'On asking bizarre questions', in M. Donaldson, R. Grieve and C. Pratt (eds) *Early Childhood Development and Education.* Oxford: Basil Blackwell Ltd.

Husen, T. (2001) 'Burrhus Frederic Skinner', in J. Palmer (ed.) *Fifty Modern Thinkers on Education.* London: Routledge.

Isaacs, S. (1999) (First published in 1930) *Intellectual Growth in Young Children.* London: Routledge and Kegan Paul.

Jenkinson, S. (2001) *The Genius of Play.* Stroud, Gloucs: Hawthorn Press.

Johnson-Laird, P. N. and Wason, P. C. (eds). (1977) *Thinking: Readings in Cognitive Science.* Cambridge: Cambridge University Press.

Kahneman, D. (2011) *Thinking Fast and Slow.* London: Allen Lane.

Karmiloff-Smith, A. (2001) 'Why babies' brains are not Swiss Army knives', in H. Rose and S. Rose (eds) *Alas Poor Darwin: Arguments Against Evolutionary Psychology.* London: Vintage.

Karmiloff, K. and Karmiloff-Smith, A. (2001) *Pathways to Language.* London: Harvard University Press.

Katz, L. (1995) *Talks with Teachers of Young Children.* Norwoord, NJ: Ablex.

Katz, L. (2011) 'Current perspectives on the early childhood curriculum', in R. House (ed.) *Too Much, Too Soon? Early Childhood and the Erosion of Childhood.* Stroud, Gloucs: Hawthorn Press.

Keenan, T. (2002) *An Introduction to Child Development.* London: Sage.

Keenan, T. and Evans, S. (2009) *An Introduction to Child Development* (2nd ed.). London: Sage.

Klein, P. (1997) 'Multiplying the Problems of Intelligence by Eight: A Critique of Gardner's Theory', Canadian Journal of Education, 22(4): 377–94.

Kohn, A. (1999) *Punished by Rewards.* New York: Houghton Mifflin Company.

Kolb. D.A. and Fry, R. (1975) 'Toward an applied theory of experiential learning', in C. Cooper (ed.) *Theories of Group Process.* London: John Wiley.

Kornhaber, M. (2001) 'Howard Gardner 1943–', in J. Palmer (ed.) *Fifty Modern Thinkers on Education: From Piaget to the Present.* London: Routledge.

Kraemer, S. (1999) 'Promoting Resilience: Changing Concepts of Parenting and Child Care', International Journal of Child and Family Welfare, 3: 273–87.

Kress, G. (1997) *Before Writing: Rethinking the Paths to Literacy.* London: Routledge.

Krechevsky, M., and Seidel, S. (1998) 'Minds at Work: Applying Multiple Intelligences in the Classroom', In R. J. Sternberg and W. M. Williams (eds.) *Intelligence, Instruction, and Assessment: Theory into Practice.* Mahwah, N.J.: Erlbaum.

Lave, J. (1988) *Cognition in Practice: Mind, Mathematics and Culture in Everyday Life.* Cambridge: Cambridge University Press.

LeDoux, J. (1998) *The Emotional Brain.* London: Weidenfeld and Nicolson.

Lee, T. (2011) 'The wisdom of Vivian Gussin Paley', in L. Miller and L. Pound (eds) *Theories and Approaches to Learning in the Early Years.* London: Sage.

Lewis-Williams, D. (2002) *The Mind in the Cave.* London: Thames and Hudson.

Lucas, B. (2001) *Power up Your Mind.* London: Nicholas Brealey Publishing.

MacNaughton, G. (2003) *Shaping Early Childhood.* Maidenhead: Open University Press.

MacNaughton, G. (2004) 'The Politics of Logic in Early Childhood Research: A Case of the Brain, Hard Facts, Trees and Rhizomes', The Australian Educational Researcher, 31, 3 December.

Malloch, S. and Trevarthen, C. (2009) *Communicative Musicality.* Oxford: Oxford University Press.

Martin, D. (2012) **www.nytimes.com/2012/02/26/us/ulric-neisser-who-reshaped-thinking-on-the-mind-dies-at-83.html?pagewanted=all** Accessed 23 May 2012.

Matthews, J. (2003) *Drawing and Painting: Children and Visual Representation* (2nd ed.). London: Paul Chapman Publishing.

Meltzoff, A. (2004) 'The case for developmental cognitive science: theories of people and things', in G. Bremner and A. Slater (eds) *Theories of Infant Development.* Oxford: Blackwell Publishing Ltd.

Millar, S. (1968) *The Psychology of Play.* Harmondsworth: Penguin Press.

Miller, G. (2003) 'The Cognitive Revolution: A Historical Perspective', *Trends in Cognitive Sciences,* 7 (3) 141–44, 1 March.

Mischel, W., Ayduk, O., Berman, M., Casey, B., Gotlib, I., Jonides, J., Kross, E., Teslovich, T., Wilson, N., Zayas, V. and Shoda, Y. (2011) '"Willpower" Over the Life Span: Decomposing Self-regulation', *Social Cognitive and Affective Neuroscience,* 6 (2): 252–56. **http://scan.oxfordjournals.org/content/6/2/252.short** Accessed 31 May 2012.

Mithen, S. (1996) *Prehistory of the Mind.* London: Thames and Hudson.

Mithen, S. (2005) *The Singing Neanderthals.* London: Weidenfeld and Nicolson.

Montessori, M. (1989) *Child, Society and the World.* Oxford: Clio Press.

Moylett, H. and Stewart, N. (2012) *Understanding the Revised Early Years Foundation Stage.* London: Early Education.

NACCCE (1999) *All our Futures: Creativity, Culture and Education.* Sudbury: DfEE Publications.

Neisser, U. (1967) *Cognitive Psychology.* New York: Appleton Century-Crofts.

Neisser, U. (1976) *Cognition and Reality.* Reading: W.H. Freeman and Co.

Nicholls, J. and Wells, G. (1985) 'Editors' Introduction', in G. Wells and J. Nicholls (eds) *Language and Learning: An Interactional Perspective.* Lewes, E. Sussex: Falmer Publishing.

Nisbett, R. (2003) *The Geography of Thought*. London: Nicholas Brealey Publishing.

Nutbrown, C. (2011) *Threads of Thinking* (4th ed.). London: Sage.

Pahl, K. (1999) *Transformations: Making Meaning in Nursery Education*. Stoke on Trent: Trentham Books.

Paley, V.G. (1990) *The Boy Who Would be a Helicopter*. London: Harvard University Press.

Paley, V.G. (2004) *A Child's Work: The Importance of Fantasy Play*. London: The University of Chicago Press.

Palmer, S. (2006) *Toxic Childhood: How Modern Life is Damaging our Children*. London: Orion Books.

Palmer, S. (2011) 'If I wanted my child to learn to read and write I wouldn't start from here', in R. House (ed.) *Too Much, Too Soon? Early Learning and the Erosion of Childhood*. Stroud, Gloucs: Hawthorn Press.

Panksepp, J. and Trevarthen, C. (2009) 'The neuroscience of emotion in music', in S. Malloch and C. Trevarthen (eds) *Communicative Musicality*. Oxford: Oxford University Press.

Papousek, H. (1994) 'To the evolution of human musicality and musical education', in I. Deliège (ed.) Proceedings of the 3rd International Conference on Music Perception and Cognition. Liège: ESCOM.

Penn, H. (2005) *Understanding Early Childhood*. Maidenhead: Open University Press.

Piaget, J. (2002) (First published in 1926) *The Language and Thought of the Child*. London: Routledge Classics.

Piaget, J. and Inhelder, B. (2007) *The Child's Conception of Space*. London: W.W. Norton and Co. (First published in English in 1957).

Pinker, S. (1994) *The Language Instinct*. London: Penguin Books.

Pollard, S. (2002) *Readings for Reflective Teaching*. London: Continuum.

Pound, L. (2005) *How Children Learn*. London: Step Forward Publishing Ltd.

Pound, L. (2008) *How Children Learn 2*. London: Practical Pre-school Books.

Pound, L. (2009) *How Children Learn 3*. London: Practical Pre-School Books.

Pound, L. (2011) *Influencing Early Childhood*. Maidenhead: McGraw-Hill.

Pound, L. and Harrison, C. (2003) *Supporting Musical Development in the Early Years*. Buckingham: Open University Press.

Pound, L. and Lee, T. (2011) *Teaching Mathematics Creatively*. London: Routledge.

Pound, L. and Miller, L. (2011) 'Critical issues', in L. Miller and L. Pound (eds) *Theories and Approaches to Learning in the Early Years*. London: Sage.

Pugh, G. (2002) 'The consequences of inadequate investment in the early years', in J. Fisher (ed.) *The Foundations of Learning*. Buckingham: Open University Press.

Ramachandran, V.S. and Blakeslee, S. (1999) *Phantoms in the Brain*. London: Fourth Estate.

Ramachandran, V.S. (2011) *The Tell-tale Brain*. London: William Heinemann.

Reddy, V. (2008) *How Infants Know Minds*. London: Harvard University Press.

Ridley, M. (2003) *Nature via Nurture: Genes, Experience and What Makes us Human*. London: Harper Perennials.

Rinaldi, C. (2001) 'Documentation and assessment: what is the relationship?', in C. Guidici, C. Rinaldi and M. Krechevsky (eds) *Making Learning Visible*. Reggio: Project Zero and Reggio Children.

Rizzolatti, G., Fogassi, L. and Gallese, V. (2006) 'Mirrors In The Mind', Scientific American, 295, 54–61.

Robinson, K. (2010) **www.ted.com/talks/ken_robinson_changing_education_paradigms.html**

Robinson, K. (2011) *Out of our Minds: Learning to be Creative*. Chichester: Capstone Publishing Ltd.

Robson, S. (2012) 'Children's experience of creative thinking?' in H. Fumoto, S. Robson, S. Greenfield, and D. Hargeaves, *Young Children's Creative Thinking*. London: Sage.

Rogers, C. (1983) *Freedom to Learn for the 80s*. New York: Merril.

Rogoff, B. (1990) *Apprenticeship in Thinking: Cognitive Development in Social Context*. Oxford: Oxford University Press.

Rogoff, B. (2002) *Learning Together: Children and Adults in a School Community*. Oxford: Oxford University Press.

Rogoff, B. (2003) *The Cultural Nature of Human Development*. Oxford: Oxford University Press.

Rose, S. (2001) 'Escaping evolutionary psychology', in H. Rose and S. Rose, *Alas Poor Darwin: Arguments Against Evolutionary Psychology*. London: Vintage.

Rose, H. and Rose, S. (2001) *Alas Poor Darwin: Arguments Against Evolutionary Psychology*. London: Vintage.

Sawyer, K., John-Stiner, V., Moran, S., Sternberg, R., Feldman, D., Nakamura, J. and Czikszentmihalyi, M. (2003) *Creativity and Development*. Oxford: Oxford University Press.

Schweinhart, L., Montie, J., Xiang, Z., Barnett, W., Blefield, C. and Nores, M. (2005) *Lifetime Effects: the HighScope Perry Preschool Study Through Age 40*. Ypsilanti, MI: HighScope Press.

Siegel, D. (1999) *The Developing Mind*. New York: The Guilford Press.

Singer, D. and Singer, J. (1990) *The House of Make-Believe*. London: Harvard University Press.

Skinner, B. (1991) [first published 1957] *Verbal Behaviour*. London: Copley Publishing Group.

Slater, L. (2004) *Opening Skinner's Box*. London: Bloomsbury Publishing plc.

Sloboda, J. (1985) *The Musical Mind*. Oxford: Oxford University Press.

Sloboda, J. and Davidson, J. (1996) 'The Young Performing Musician', in: I. Deliege, and Sloboda, J. (eds) *Musical beginnings*. Oxford: Oxford University Press.

Smidt, S. (2009) *Introducing Vygotsky*. London: Routledge.

Smith, A. (2011) 'Relationships with people, places and things: Te Whariki', in L. Miller and L. Pound (eds) *Theories and Approaches to Learning in the Early Years*. London: Sage.

Steiner, R. (1907) (1996) *The Education of the Child*. Hudson, NY: Anthroposophic Press.

Sternberg, R. (1985) *Beyond IQ: A Triarchic Theory of Human Intelligence*. Cambridge: Cambridge University Press.

Sternberg, R. (1990) *Metaphors of Mind: Conceptions of the Nature of Intelligence*. Cambridge: Cambridge University Press.

Sternberg, R. (1997) 'The Concept of Intelligence and its Role in Lifelong Learning and Success', American Psychologist, Vol 52 (10), Oct, 1030–37.

Sternberg, R. and Detterman, D. (eds) (1986) *What is Intelligence? Contemporary Viewpoints on its Nature and Conception*. Norwood, NJ: Ablex.

Sternberg, R., Conway, B., Ketron, J. and Bernstein, M. (1981) 'People's Conception of Intelligence', Journal of Personality and Social Psychology, 41: 37–55.

Stewart, N. (2012) *How Children Learn: The Characteristics of Effective Early Learning*. London: Early Education.

Suggate, S. (2011) 'Viewing the long-term effects of early reading with an open eye', in R. House (ed.) *Too much, Too Soon? Early Learning and the Erosion of Childhood*. Stroud, Gloucs: Hawthorn Press.

Surowieck, J. (2004) *The Wisdom of Crowds*. New York: Doubleday.

Swain, F. (2011) 3 August 2011 'Susan Greenfield: Living online is changing our brains', New Scientist. **www.newscientist.com/article/mg21128236.400-susan-greenfield-living-online-is-changing-our-brains.html.** Retrieved 12 June 2012.

Swann, W. (1985) 'Psychological science and the practice of special education', in G. Claxton, W. Swann, P. Salmon, V. Walkerdine, B. Jacobsen and J. White, *Psychology and Schooling: What's the Matter?* London: Bedford Way Papers.

Talay-Ongan, A. (1998) Typical and Atypical Development in Early Childhood. Leicester: The British Psychological Society.

Thelen, E. and Adolph, K. (1992) 'Arnold L. Gesell: The Paradox of Nature and Nurture', Developmental Psychology, 28(3): 368–80.

Tobin, J. (2004) 'The disappearance of the body in early childhood education', in L. Bresler (ed) *Knowing Bodies, Moving Minds: Towards Embodied Teaching and Learning.* London: Kluwer Academic Publishers.

Tovey, H. (2007) *Playing Outdoors.* Maidenhead: Open University Press.

Trevarthen, C. (2008) 'Intuition for human communication', in M. Zeedyk (ed.) *Promoting Social Interaction for Individuals with Communication Impairment.* London: Jessica Kingsley Publishers.

Trevarthen, C. (2011) 'What Is It Like To Be a Person Who Knows Nothing? Defining the Active Intersubjective Mind of a Newborn Human Being', Infant and Child Development, 20(1) 119–135 Jan/Feb.

Trevarthen, C. and Marwick, H. (2002) *Review of Childcare and the Development of Children Aged 0–3: Research Evidence and Implications for Out-of-home Provision.* Edinburgh; Scottish Executive.

Vargas, J. (2005) *A Brief Biography of B. F. Skinner* **www.bfskinner.org/bfskinner/AboutSkinner.html** Accessed 16 May 2012.

Vygotsky, L. (1978) *Mind in Society.* Cambridge MA: Harvard University Press.

Walsh, D. (2004) 'Frog boy and the American monkey: the body in Japanese early schooling', in L. Bresler (ed.) *Knowing Bodies, Moving Minds: Towards Embodied Teaching and Learning.* London: Kluwer Academic Publishers.

Wells, G. and Nicholls, J. (1985) (eds) *Language and Learning: An Interactional Perspective.* Lewes, E. Sussex: Falmer Publishing.

White, J. (2008) *Playing and Learning Outdoors.* London: Routledge/Nursery World.

White, J. (2008) 'Illusory Intelligence', Journal of the Philosophy of Education, 42(3–4): 611–30 Aug/Nov.

Willingham, D.T. (2009). 'Three Problems in the Marriage of Neuroscience and Education', Cortex, 45 (4): 544–45.

Wood, D., Bruner, J. and Ross, G. (1976) 'The Role of Tutoring in Problem-solving', Journal of Child Psychiatry and Psychology, 17(2): 89–100 **http://onlinelibrary.wiley.com/doi/10.1111/j.1469-7610.1976.tb00381.x/abstract**

Index